D0287822

AMATEUR NIGHT AT THE APOLLO

Portrait of the author, 1940

AMATEUR NIGHT AT THE APOLLO

★ ★

RALPH COOPER PRESENTS FIVE DECADES OF GREAT ENTERTAINMENT

RALPH COOPER

with STEVE DOUGHERTY

HarperCollins*Publishers*

FIRST EDITION

Designer: Helene Berinsky

Library of Congress Cataloging-in-Publication Data

Cooper, Ralph, 1918-
    Amateur night at the Apollo : Ralph Cooper presents five decades
of great entertainment / Ralph Cooper, Steve Dougherty.—1st ed.
        p. cm.
    ISBN 0-06-016037-3
    1. Apollo Theatre (New York, N.Y.) 2. Afro-Americans—New York
(N.Y.)—Music—History and criticism. 3. Popular music—New York
(N.Y.)—History and criticism. I. Dougherty, Steve, 1948-
II. Title.
ML3479.C66 1990
792.7'09747'1—dc20   89-46522

90 91 92 93 94 CG/MP 10 9 8 7 6 5 4 3 2 1

Black artists in the pursuit of their profession, unlike their white counterparts, were subjected to insults, deprivation, and unbelievable hardship. Their only companion, support, and confidant was their passionate dedication to their respective talents. I, therefore, have chosen to dedicate this book to five artists whose struggle to attain stardom mirrors a hallmark incentive to all young, talented future stars.

—Ralph Cooper

Marian Anderson

Bert Williams

Josephine Baker, 1951

Florence Mills

Paul Robeson

Contents

★ ★

Foreword

★ ★

There is an old adage "Truth is stranger than fiction." You are about to embark on a journey, as you read this book, that will prove that adage true.

It is the story of a warrior—a man who unselfishly put his race above all else and made changes.

It is the story of a creative genius—a man who has touched and launched more careers than any one person ever in the world.

It is a story of American history—if we learn where we have come from, what we are responsible for, maybe we can grasp where we are going.

It is a story of inspiration and imagination.

It is a story of energy.

It is a story of love and a lesson for all of us in giving, for those are part of the elements that helped shape the vision that Ralph Cooper saw.

As a child growing up in my father's house I was privy to a world that most would find hard to imagine. At the age of four I was my dad's shadow, wherever he went I was his companion. This enabled me to know all the stars of the day as well as the VIPs—who

I thought of as my aunts and uncles. Marian Anderson actually is my godmother.

Our house was a cultural haven. Art was everywhere—living art. People such as Count Basie, Floyd Patterson, Muhammad Ali, Duke Ellington, and others were frequent visitors at the home of my dad and mom, singer Betti Mays.

This is a true story of travels, trials, tribulations, and triumphs. The humblest man I know, the quietest man I know, deserves the respect of letting the world know how it all started.

Dad, I love you.

Enjoy your journey.

RALPH COOPER II

AMATEUR NIGHT AT THE APOLLO

There's Been a Whole Lotta Quaking Goin' On

★ ★

In the northern part of Manhattan, there is a crack in the earth's crust known as the 125th Street Fault Line. It is a deep, jagged fissure in the granite rock formation that runs under Harlem's teeming Main Street, from the island's West Side at the Hudson River, all the way across town to the gentler shores of the East River.

Geologists say that an earthquake could split the Big Apple in two by the year 2010—which means 125th Street beach property might not be a bad investment after all. When the Big One hits, Harlem will be *the* place to be in New York City—the only place. Downtown will be so far down you'll need a submarine to cruise Wall Street.

That would suit folks uptown just fine. But there is one problem.

If the city starts to shake and rattle any Wednesday between sundown and who knows when after midnight, nobody uptown will notice it. Because every Wednesday for most of the past fifty years the 125th Street Apollo Theatre has been host to Ralph Cooper's Original Harlem Amateur Night. And no matter how much quaking Mr. Richter's scale picks up outside the theatre, nobody will feel it for all the seismic shaking going on inside.

There has never been anything else in show business quite like my Harlem Amateur Night. Ever since the autumn of 1934, when I first encouraged a dozen fear-stricken amateur contestants to stand trial at the Apollo before fifteen hundred of the smartest, most boisterous hanging judges ever convened, the chemistry on Amateur Nights has been explosive. Pick a Wednesday, any Wednesday, to make the scene at the Apollo and I personally guarantee you'll see more talents, more high drama and comedy than you'd get in a month of Broadway shows.

Anyone who has read about hubris in old books can watch it work on the Apollo stage, where the smug and cocky routinely crash and burn, and where the meek and trembling can surprise the world with voices full of more power and emotion than they ever guessed they had in them.

It happened to Ella Fitzgerald over fifty years ago. The future First Lady of Jazz was just a teenager then, and so scared she almost blew the performance that launched her career. Nearly half a century later, a terrified kid named Luther Vandross got booed off our stage four times before he finally won over the crowd. If he hadn't been dedicated enough to come back for a fifth try, the soul star would be just as meek and unknown now as he was then.

Ella and Luther are proof of the truth: As long as there is an Amateur Night in Harlem, there will always be some brand-new nobody with the chutzpah to stand on our stage and dare to be somebody.

Not since the groundlings at the Globe booed Shakespeare has an audience been as feared—or as much fun to be a part of. Mae West liked to go to the Apollo to boo her lusty best. Joan Crawford came to practice her dramatic screeching. And Milton Berle, Jackie Gleason, Humphrey Bogart, and Marilyn Monroe all did their share of hollering. In more recent years, such heavyweight superstars as Jesse Jackson, Andy Warhol, Mike Tyson, Robin Givens, Gloria Steinem, Bill Cosby, Vanessa Williams, and Sugar Ray Leonard regularly get in on the hell raising.

Amateur Night audiences don't express themselves by pelting runoffs with rotten tomatoes and spoiled eggs. Our crowd summons a grinning demon with its displeasure. Our infamous Executioner, portrayed by the very talented C. P. Lacey, is part genie, part clown, and part angel of death. It's his job to put the booed and the hissed out of their misery; and he does it with much perverse glee, to the rollicking delight of the crowd.

But the audience is not out only to condemn lost souls to everlasting anonymity. The whistles and cheers of praise delivered by that same cutthroat crowd are the heavenly sounds every contestant prays for. Only a gifted few know what it's like to be anointed by Apollo Theatre applause. For them, it's like winning the lottery on their wedding day. Nothing tops it—except the payoff—the road to success.

As all our contestants know, stars as legendary as Ella and Luther, Sarah Vaughan, Gladys Knight, and Michael Jackson were unknowns before they won the approval of the dangerous, high-voltage Harlem Amateur Night audience. Perhaps one of the next *century's* great stars will begin to shine on the Apollo stage tonight.

Tomorrow's Stars Today!

★ ★

More than an hour before showtime, the crowd begins to gather on the 125th Street sidewalk beneath the Apollo Theatre marquee. Overhead the promise is written in lights: TOMORROW'S STARS TODAY! *RALPH COOPER PRESENTS AMATEUR NIGHT AT THE APOLLO!*

Tonight is the biggest night of our year, our annual Super Dog contest, when we invite the top amateur winners from the past year to compete for a three-thousand-dollar grand prize and the near-legal-tender title of Amateur of the Year. Tickets have been sold out for months, and the atmosphere outside the theatre is as electric as Hollywood on Academy Awards night.

Like the zoot-suited Amateur Night fans of years ago, these early arrivals look their show-stopping best, sporting everything from floor-length minks, silk dusters, and lawyerly dark suits to hip-hopster gold chains, designer turtlenecks and baggy pants. By the door a couple of dudes in leather pastel jackets, with thick, heavy-duty braids of gold draped around their necks, are making time with two gorgeous, long-stemmed damsels. One is wrapped up like a present with a big satin bow on her backside, and both wear the shortest, tightest, tini-

"SOLD OUT." As much as folks in need of a ticket hate to hear it, that phrase has always turned me on—and it's a phrase I enjoy hearing almost every Wednesday.

est, miniest miniskirts allowable by the laws of nature. All it takes is a stroll outside the Apollo to prove that the women of today are just as "tall, tan, and terrific" as the beautiful flapper "frails" of yesteryear. Oh, and do dig those new, high-style scalps! Half the guys out here tonight are walking around with hair art on their heads. Today's barber not only has to know how to cut hair—he's got to be able to create sculpture with his razor.

Ticket sales for future shows are all that's being transacted at the box office. But the hopes of the ticketless aren't dead, as long as they got the bread. Any number of the "independent ticket brokers" hanging in the shadows might be talked out of a twelve-dollar balcony seat for twenty-five, or a fifteen-dollar orchestra seat for a whole lot more.

Eddie Murphy and Gregory Hines are among the celebrities.

Traffic has slowed to a loud jam of cabs and limos and hired cars, all trying to maneuver as close as possible to the theatre entrance. Half a block west on 125th Street, stuck in the middle of all the tied-up city traffic like a pair of mastodons in the mud flats, are two tour buses ferrying German and Japanese tourists from their expensive midtown hotels to the Apollo, an important American cultural landmark on the itinerary of thousands of foreign tourists each year.

As the buses inch their way toward the marquee, snippets of rap, funk, and pop boom from beat boxes and from passing cars that blast so loud they sound equipped with audio artillery. Even the cops on crowd-control duty on 125th Street are caught up in the rhythm, shifting their weight foot to foot as they stand hip hop. Across the street, moving and grooving right along to the beat, is a posse of homeboys who throw their hands in the air, twist their hips, and do the Worm while watching the Amateur Night crowd gather and begin to move into the theatre.

Once through the theatre's tall glass doors, ticket holders enter a long white, high-ceilinged, gilded passageway steeped in show-business history.

The broad hall leading to a row of heavy brass doors and the famed auditorium beyond is lined with color-tinted photo murals that make up the theatre's ''Wall of Fame.'' Generations of show-business greats—Bessie Smith, Louis Armstrong, Count Basie, Louis Jordan, Charlie Parker, Miles Davis, Otis Redding, Stevie Wonder, Diana Ross, the Jackson 5, and many others whose stars shined brightly from the Apollo stage—smile upon and inspire the procession. For some, the message is obvious. Many of the artists pictured began their careers as Amateur Night contestants. And tonight, they know, some new legend may be born.

Science has not yet established when, exactly, the average Apollo ticket holder sheds his or her normal, workaday identity and becomes part of the smartest, rowdiest, hell-raisingest, and most knowledgeable audience in show business. The transformation may begin as soon as he or she enters the theatre and walks past the Wall of Fame or when the ticket holder is ushered to a seat in the orchestra or in one of the two balconies or one of the lower-mezzanine boxes. Most likely, the transformation takes place between the time our hot combo, the Apollo House Rockers, starts jamming at seven-thirty and when the first contestant walks weak-kneed to the microphone fifteen minutes later. Whatever the timing, be sure that the transformation is total.

At the moment, I'm in my dressing room, one flight above the stage, relaxing before the show. I don't need to get psyched hours before curtain time. I'll get wound up when it's time to go out there and pitch. Until then, I like to take it easy. I'm not the kind who needs to be alone just before show time. I like people around. I like

Amateur Night fans never know who is going to drop by to take a bow. Here Spike Lee helps me introduce an amateur contestant.

to talk and joke while I get made up and figure out what suit I'll need to look my sartorial best.

I've already sent one of my people downstairs to check out the crowd. I like to know who's out there before I go on, because whenever I'm onstage and see a celebrity in the audience, I ask him/her to stand and take a bow. It's a tradition dating back to the days when Eddie Cantor or Jackie Gleason or Jack Benny would stand up so the folks could see them. One night a few years ago there was a famous artist in the audience. He was an old friend who had been attending the amateur shows for years. But in my enthusiasm, and much to my embarrassment, I introduced my friend Paul Simon as "that great performer Neil Simon." On another night I looked up at the stage-right box and saw Tawana Brawley, center of the most controversial criminal case in recent New York history, taking in an Amateur Night show when public furor about her case was at its peak. I asked her to take a bow, but Tawana kept her seat. Tonight's Super Dog contest has attracted some celebrated figures, including Spike Lee, Keith Sweat, and the rappers Big Daddy Kane and Jam Master Jay of Run-D.M.C.

I can hear the House Rockers pumping all the way upstairs, and from everything I'm told, it looks like tonight is going to be another wild one. The crowd is already keyed up and raucous. My son and associate producer, Ralph II, says there is a row of fraternity guys in the rear orchestra seats braying like drunken hounds—"WOOF WOOF WOOF WOOF WOOF." Up in the balconies, the girls are shaking their money-makers, the B-boys are swaying and rocking on the beat—and the show hasn't even started yet.

In 1989, two champs, Mike Tyson and the reigning Miss America, Debbie Turner, brought the house down when I invited them to take a bow on Amateur Night.

Folks are seven deep at all the bars; a group of girls are doing Da Butt in an aisle downstairs; and in the orchestra seats, the German and Japanese tourists wear the slightly worried, disoriented looks of people who have wandered into the midst of a lion's den.

But the tourists' discomfort is pure adrenal joy compared to the heart-pounding anxiety being suffered right now by the tortured souls

I tried to get Sugar Ray Leonard to do some dancing outside the ring.

1989 was the year the New Kids on the Block went through the roof. They began the year with a guest appearance at Club Apollo, where the Amateur Night audience loved lead singer Joe McIntyre and his buddies from Boston.

crammed into the stifling, overcrowded Green Room, located directly below the stage in the bowels of the theatre.

Despite the installation of a brand-new air-conditioning and heating system that keeps the rest of the theatre comfortable year round, the Green Room always feels hot, thanks to the fitful, collective breath of three dozen fear-stricken contestants and their guests, who compete for twenty or so folding aluminum chairs set up in front of a pair of new television monitors. For the amateur hopefuls whose long-awaited shot at stardom has finally arrived, tonight is the biggest—and scariest—night of their lives. They began arriving at the backstage, 126th Street entrance hours earlier, making their way to the theatre by subway, bus, and car from neighborhoods in the five boroughs, as well as upstate New York, New Jersey, Connecticut, and Long Island. One group of singers has driven in from Harrisburg, Pennsylvania, and another from Washington, D.C., supported by three busloads of fans.

But there is little inclination for the contestants to get to know one another. All who enter the Green Room abandon any hope for a relaxed, anxiety-free evening among friends. Pure, undiluted, knee-buckling, gut-wrenching, breath-stealing fear is the common thread that joins all contestants in a brotherhood of fright. Anyone who ever has been shot out of a cannon, has rappeled from the top of the Empire State Building, or has jumped from the bomb bay of a F-14 at thirty thousand feet has an idea what it is like for the amateurs down in the Green Room, rehearsing lines, making emergency costume repairs, and counting seconds until curtain time. "Agony" is not too strong a word. The only relief is provided by a soft-drink machine (seventy-five cents, quarters only) and a pair of tiny, single-seat bathrooms.

Sometimes I go down to the Green Room before the show to give the kids a little encouragement on their way to triumph or doom. All you have to do is step into that room and you can feel the sweaty palms, the knotted stomachs, the jellied knees, and the pounding hearts. In the long line for the men's room I find a bright and desperate young man I've known for years, named Barry Manderson. Barry wants to be a singer and dancer. But he reads the phone book for a living—he's a proofreader. He's also living proof that the mere threat of getting booed is enough to make a strong man weak in the knees and sick in the stomach. Short, squat, and powerful, Barry looks like he could take Tyson—"for a subway ride," at least. Barry has already survived several rounds on the regular Amateur Night, and he's even won a few. A wimp he definitely is not. But, like a fighter who's been punched one too many times, Barry is jumpy. He can remember being booed offstage during an amateur competition a couple of years ago.

"How you doing, Barry?" I say when I see him.

"Hello, Mr. Cooper. I don't feel so good."

"Don't worry, son—you'll do fine tonight. Get out there and kill 'em."

Finally the bathroom is free and Barry rushes in. When he gets out, he apologizes for his hurry. Embarrassed, he tells me he had an attack of diarrhea. Of course I can't resist: "Oh, well," I say, "when you gotta run, you gotta run."

David Sanborn and Al Jarreau have a few tips for Amateur sax man Amani Murray.

Even though Barry knows that one of his favorite singers, Otis Redding, sat and suffered under the same roof, he finds no comfort in the knowledge. And so Barry prays—over and over, the same prayer: "Thank you, Lord, for the gifts you have given me. If it is meant to be, then I know it is your will."

Barry's aren't the only prayers being muttered in the Green Room tonight. Over by the soda machine I meet Privacy, a vocal trio of three pretty girls who are rehearsing the song they plan to sing tonight: "Secret Lady," the hit by Stephanie Mills who they know, was eleven when she won Amateur Night. "Stephanie sang a Stevie Wonder song, 'For Once in My Life,' " one of the girls says, as if by reciting the information she can gain strength from it. The Privacy girls—Sheryle, Kim, and Terry—are about twenty years old, and they

Like many other stars who got their start on our stage, Patti LaBelle still can't get enough of that famous Apollo audience.

Whitney Houston, whose aunt Dionne Warwick was an Amateur Night winner, entertained the Apollo's troops in 1986.

14

say they've been rehearsing Stephanie's song every night for the past month. They know the song inside and out, but still they worry about their confidence, and so they pray for that.

"Sometimes," Sheryle says, "I think there are people in the audience who are just out to get me."

"No," I say. "They want you to be great. They only boo if you're not."

I make my way across the Green Room floor, stepping over the outstretched legs of limbering dancers and around gargling singers to the spiral staircase that climbs to the stage-left wing. At the top of the spiral, I nearly trip over a thirty-five-inch talent—a young man named Brian Goins. Brian is five, the age his big brother Tony was eleven years ago when he entered Amateur Night to sing "Call HIM Up and Tell HIM What You Want." That has to be the best gospel novelty song ever written. And coming from a five-year-old, the song, which is about how God's phone line is never busy, was more novel than ever. Now Tony and Brian and three other brothers have formed a group, called, fittingly, Fam-Lee. Their mom, Debra, is the band's manager, agent, publicist, accountant, costume designer, and toughest critic. Music is in the boys' blood. Debra's brother was Glen Goins, the lead singer for George Clinton's Parliament-Funkadelic, who died much too young at twenty-four.

The Goinses are about as close to being a professional amateur act as you can get. Debra told me once that she sold all her living-room furniture, turned her living room into her dining room, and turned the old dining room into a fully equipped recording studio and rehearsal hall. She runs her family with one goal in mind: "To make Fam-Lee the next Jackson Five." Seeing little Brian practice his knee drops behind the big curtains is almost enough to make a believer of me.

None of the Fam-Lee members notice the young man back behind the scenery flats changing into his Executioner costume. The man who haunts every amateur's worst nightmares is in real life a kindhearted and enormously talented young comedian, singer, and dancer named C. P. Lacey. For my money, he's the best Executioner we've had ever since my original Executioner, Porto Rico.

Getting dressed is an hour-long project for Lacey, who wears two other costumes underneath his Executioner gear. First he pulls on the skintight James Brown suit he will strip down to for the bring-

A lady with her own kind of soul, Dolly Parton wowed 'em at the Apollo, where she joined me onstage. I doubt Dolly ever heard a more enthusiastic audience, even at her own Grand Ole Opry theatre down in Nashville.

the-house-down finale, when he sings "Please, Please, Please," with all the jumps and leg splits James does. (Some nights I think Lacey is James Brown.) Over that suit, Lacey drapes himself in the leather-and-chains outfit he uses in his crotch-grabbing routine as Michael Jackson singing "Man in the Mirror." Somehow, Lacey wears all those layers of stuff and still manages to look as skinny as Michael himself. Now, as I walk over to say hello, Lacey is busy with the final, top layer of his costume. Every week Lacey creates a new look, and this installment is Rasta Man, the Killer Clown.

"Tonight is going to be crazy," Lacey says, pulling on a pair of shiny yellow rubber boots and wiggling into a green grass skirt, a Hawaiian shirt, and a red fright wig braided into dreadlocks.

Just then the House Rockers wind up their opening miniconcert

Ben Vereen used to dream about dancing onstage at the Apollo.

to a rave finish. Now Ralph II takes over and builds the excitement until a roar lets loose in the theatre that must stop the heart of every amateur in the building.

"And now, ladies and gentlemen," he says, "the legendary creator, star, and host of Harlem Amateur Night, the one and only Mr. RALPH COOPER!"

I make my usual entrance, which is really *un*usual. I can only describe it as a customized street dance, complete with push-offs, a bambolina twist, a wild funky glide, and—just to show the kids in the balconies a thing or two—a moonwalk, a move that always gets a rise out of my audience.

You must understand that the Apollo audience and I have always had a magical rapport, a real love for each other. Maybe it's because

Amateur contestant
Tony Quartermain
gives it his all.

Stephanie Mills was eleven
when she became an Ama-
teur Night winner. She is a
big inspiration to our young
contestants.

I trust them to tell it like it is and they trust me because they know I care for them. I don't really know why we love each other or what the cause of it is; but then I don't know the scientific explanation of why I love my wife—I just do.

Contestants sometimes don't like to hear me say this, but I don't ever remember a time when I was nervous in this theatre. It's strange. Many professional show people walk out in front of this audience scared. And when they do, the audience senses it and eats 'em alive.

It's not difficult to understand why it's such a shock to the nervous system to walk out into the spotlight. Standing on the wide wooden stage of the Apollo, the theatre seems tiny—and scary. The packed balconies loom close behind the footlights. They seem to rise high and straight up out of the floor. Standing onstage, you feel like you can stretch an arm and touch the people in the last row of the second balcony—or they can reach down and slap you right offstage. The mezzanine boxes hang so low and close to the stage, John Wilkes Booth would have had no trouble making the leap. While the red velvet Chinese curtains, the gold filigree on the white woodwork, and the gorgeous crystal chandeliers create a warm and intimate theatre glow, it's up to each contestant who walks onstage to determine whether he is standing in theatre heaven or show-business hell.

But I've always had a good feeling on this stage. It seems to me this stage is where I was born to be. *Time* magazine says the audience is the lion and I'm the lion tamer. "You gotta be out of your mind to walk into that lion's cage," I've been told. "A lot of people walk out on that stage and get et." Well, I ain't been "et" yet.

Before I invite the first volunteer into the cage, I introduce the show. "Welcome, ladies and gentlemen, to Ralph Cooper's world-famous Original Amateur Night, the show that is often imitated but never duplicated. We have got a real exciting, unusual show tonight, ladies and gentlemen. The main thing is to enjoy yourselves. We have some wonderful young talent here. All winners throughout the year. If you love 'em, show 'em. Make some noise. But if you think they need a little woodsheddin'—don't be afraid to let 'em know that, too!"

The audience gives a big, nerve-rattling cheer to the first contestant, a tall young man who makes the short walk from the wings to the center-stage mike with a look of such fear in his eyes, you'd swear he was going to Sing Sing, not just to sing. A nineteen-year-old from Piscataway, New Jersey, the kid looks scared, but there's courage in his heart. He's wearing a brand-new white suit, and he sings a bluesy, slowed-down, and sexy version of Prince's "Alphabet City." The girls in the audience love it, and they let him know with their screams.

Down in front, at her usual place in the very first row, a center-aisle seat, the Woman in White—Eva—is on her feet, swaying to the music, waving one hand overhead, and gazing at the singer with a look of utter rapture. And she's in the same seat every week. Eva never stands for losers, so as soon as I see her on her feet and swaying, I know Piscataway Pete won't get a visit from Lacey tonight. Sure enough, Pete floats offstage on a wave of good cheers; and when I call him back to take a bow, I can almost hear the giant sigh of relief rolling up from the Green Room.

But any below who think Pete's good fortune means that the audience's brute reputation is a lot of hype best beware.

As if by some demonic design, the second act, a sweet, tiny little girl in a blue ball gown, doesn't get through the first bar of her Anita Baker song before the booing begins in the second balcony. It's a shaky start; but I'm pulling for her, because I remember her winning performance and I know she can do it. And for a minute it looks good for her. She was smart enough to invite a few of her friends to cheer her on, and they're doing just that, from their seats in the first balcony. They applaud with enough gusto to delay the inevitable through the first chorus.

But their enthusiasm never spreads through the house; and halfway through the second chorus, the booing fills the theatre and I signal Jimmy Benjamin. It's Jimmy's job to crank the handle that operates the old-fashioned air-raid siren. A kind of aural hook, the siren is a not-too-subtle way of informing the contestant that his or her services are no longer required. At the same time, the damn thing is loud enough to wake the dead for miles around.

But the girl sings on, through the boos and despite the fact that the siren is so loud she's covering her ears with her hands in order to hear herself sing. Unfortunately, she's the only person in the theatre who cares to listen.

Still, she sings on. This is a common reaction to the boos and the siren, a futile form of what psycholgists call denial. She is denying the reality she hears and sees all around her.

Comedian Greg Cooper is no relation, but he was funny enough to tie for first place in 1989.

Certainly, there's no way she can miss the ladies in the second and third rows rocking back and forth in their seats, hooting with laughter. Nor can she help wondering why the Woman in White is writhing in agony. Instead of standing, Eva twists in her seat to avert her eyes, which are shut tight to make sure that no glimpse of the performer can creep into her vision. At the same time, she holds one hand in front of her face and flits it in a sort of backhand wave at the singer, as if trying to shoo her offstage.

But none of this gets through to the girl, who keeps on singing—perhaps because she's focusing on the German tourists in the center-orchestra seats. She can see that they're not booing her. But they're not applauding, either.

It's clear to me that the Germans haven't quite gotten into the swing of things yet. They still look a bit bewildered, sitting there as stiff as—well, Germans. The Japanese, by contrast, already have the hang of it. They're all on their feet jeering, waving their arms, jumping up and down and shouting "HAI!" instead, perhaps, of "BOO!"

Suddenly, an orange-and-yellow blur—the Executioner—comes hurtling across stage from the singer's left. Like a cartoon cannonball he stops dead, abruptly and implausibly, several yards from the microphone, where the singer gasps her last lyric and the crowd erupts with laughter. The Executioner sniffs the air, smells something foul, frowns, and holds his nose, pointing at the singer, who seems rooted to her spot, unable to move. Now Lacey pulls a gigantic pistol from his belt and levels it at the girl, who still stands, as if paralyzed. The drummer cracks off a few rim shots as Lacey plugs the hapless singer, who drops the microphone to the floor but still refuses, in her shock, to budge. Lacey, of course, is ready for this. He pulls a short-handled broom from his waistband and starts to sweep the poor girl from the stage. Now she speed-walks offstage as Lacey's broom flicks at her feet. I can see tears streaming from her eyes as she hustles past me and runs downstairs to the Green Room, where waiting contestants will treat her like she has the plague, since it's considered bad luck to befriend a loser. No one wants to be tainted on his or her big night.

Lacey seems just as unhappy about his latest duty as his victim. "I wish they didn't boo her," he says. "She was good. *I* thought so, anyway." Now he knows how Anne Boleyn's headsman must have felt. It's never easy to execute a beautiful girl.

As often happens, I think that the girl was better than the audience gave her credit for. So I give them a mild scolding for booing prematurely. "The lady is capable and can sing," I say. "She just had the bad luck of following a tough act." But the audience is not the least bit contrite. They are hungry. And the beast must be fed.

Next up is another young female singer, who emulates Melissa Morgan's "Do You Still Love Me?" The crowd doesn't; and before the song is half over, Lacey is back doing his Grim Reaper act.

The man the kids live in fear of, C. P. Lacey, our talented Amateur Night Executioner. For my money, he's the best we've had since the original, Porto Rico.

Our amateur rappers were thrilled when Biz Markie appeared
as an Amateur Night guest.

Now comes a big, clumsy man whose right foot is in a cast. The
audience has no sympathy, and Lacey returns—on crutches!—to help
him on his way to the wings. Bigfoot is followed by two rap acts, and
both get rapped by Lacey's fast disservice. "Man," mutters Daryl
Mull, one of the Apollo's talented young stagehands, "this crowd!"
It's enough to send Barry Manderson back to the toilet.

So far the pace of the show has been wild as a runaway loco-
motive. Acts are getting booed that don't deserve to be. Part of the
reason is that booing gets infectious. It's like running downhill—you
start booing and you just can't stop till you hit bottom. If I can slow
things down a little, give the audience time to catch its breath, they
might be more receptive. But the next act scheduled is shaky. I need
someone who the audience will want to cheer for. So before I go back

The ABC Dancers, who tied for first place in a 1989 contest, prove an old Amateur Night rule—you're never too young to dare.

out onstage, I ask Jackie Smith, my talent coordinator, to juggle the lineup.

"Hey, my brothers and sisters," I say to the audience. "You are on the warpath tonight! You are tough. What did you have for dinner? Y'all must have eaten the pig's foot and the shoe! Now I'm going to see just how tough you are. I'm about to bring out on this stage an act that I think is going to be a show-business giant. Ladies and gentlemen—from Plainfield, New Jersey—the Fam-Lee! Tony! Berkley! Keith! Corey! And the littlest big man of them all—Brian!"

My plan works. The audience cheers as if Michael Jackson himself was skip-running onto the stage. Little Brian, wearing a tiny tailored, sharp-creased suit, executes a quick spin, claps his hands over his head, does his knee drop, springs to his feet, spins again,

Karen Briggs fiddled while another of our talented amateurs, Karen Anderson, belted out a song during the Club Apollo portion of our show. Each week our Apollo models display their stuff in a lively fashion show. Afterwards, they enjoy the show from tables in our onstage "nightclub," which is modeled after the great clubs that used to jump at all hours throughout Harlem.

and grabs the shortest microphone onstage as his brothers step to their mikes for the start of Michael Jackson's "Who's Loving You?" Fam-Lee, with little Brian executing some hot dance steps, manages to get the entire crowd on its feet and throwing money—tons of it. Bills rain down. By the time the boys finish their number, there's over five hundred dollars scattered around the stage. Thrilled when the boys finish to resounding applause, mom Debra stands on her tiptoes and gives me a big hug and kiss. "I was so scared for them," she says. "I was really nervous. But they were wonderful."

There are some surprises waiting for the boys when they come offstage. Mike Tyson greets them with high fives and poses for photos before the Goinses head down to the Green Room. There, a bearded man approaches Tony Goins and introduces himself. Tony immediately runs upstairs. "Hey, Mom!" he hollers from the top of the stairs. "Jam Master Jay, Mom! Jam Master Jay, Mom!"

"Who is Jam Master Jay Mom?" Debra asks me.

"You know, Mom!" Tony says. "Run-D.M.C.!"

The Fam-Lee members stay downstairs to savor the best crowd response of the night. But back upstairs, the lion has not turned into a lamb. The very next act out, a young woman singer, gets booed, drops her microphone on the stage, and walks off before Lacey has a chance to execute the crowd's wishes. Now comes a solo rapper who gets the same treatment as the first two rap acts. I go back onstage with a little rap of my own. "You thought his rhyme was a crime, so you booed him off in no time."

The next act out is a four-member harmony group from Washington, D.C. Roger, the House Rockers' bandleader and pianist, reminded me earlier how good this group had been in their prior winning

The Harlem Pop Lockers take their name from one of uptown's popular hip-hop dance steps. Those are Club Apollo "models" enjoying the acrobatics in the background.

performance. "My money's on them to win the whole thing tonight," he said. But the guys look better in their matching electric blue suits than they sound. One of their microphones fades in and out, and that seems to unnerve them. The booing starts at the beginning of the first chorus; and try as they might, the singers just can't turn the audience around. The fellas do some nice steps, and their harmonies are right on; but the lead singer can't find his strongest voice, and I can see panic in his eyes as the crowd gets more and more impatient. Finally, I can put off the inevitable no longer, and I signal Jimmy B. to crank the siren.

As Lacey chases them off, a man standing next to me starts cussing, and I realize it must be their manager. "Don't blame the audience, and don't blame your boys," I say to him. "The audience says they need some work. Maybe it's not fair, but there it is. If it didn't happen tonight, it would happen somewhere down the line. All they need is to build their confidence by coming back and trying again."

Just then I notice a big-eyed girl in a white dress standing in the shadows behind the manager. Immediately I recognize Devora Weiss, a church singer from Trenton, New Jersey, who had appeared and won a few times with her beautiful gospel soul renditions. But when I say hello, she seems to tremble. "What's the matter, Devora?" I ask her, remembering nights when she left the audience limp from a spiritual number that had both balconies on their feet singing along and the Woman in White blowing kisses and crying her eyes out.

"I drove in from Trenton with a van full of people from church who came to see me sing," she says. "But I don't know if I want to go out there tonight."

"But you won two weeks ago," I said. "You're fantastic. They love you."

"No," she says. "I don't know. They're wild tonight."

When it's time to introduce her, I tell the crowd, "She can sing a while, I tell ya." And sure enough, the audience is so captivated by her rendition of "Inseparable," they do something they rarely do—namely, applaud so long and loud that Devora comes all the way back up from the Green Room to take a second bow.

The next act is the only Japanese blues singer I've ever heard. Yuki Ogiso sings the blues like I used to think only African-Americans could sing them. Yuki has long straight black hair and a wide-smiling

Oriental face. But close your eyes when he sings "Stormy Monday" and you'd never guess the singer was a Japanese who spoke broken English. The crowd is just as impressed as I am, and Yuki gets one of the biggest hands of the night.

I begin to think about sending Lacey home for the night after the E.R.E. dancers, a teenage troupe from Brooklyn led by a 250-pound youngster named Trevor who moves and flips and hops like a featherweight, win a standing ovation. But the next act out is a married couple who sing an old Marvin Gaye and Tammi Terrell song. They don't sound so bad, but they overact, and the audience pelts them with boos until Lacey appears and puts us all out of their misery.

During their number, I notice Barry Manderson sitting on the floor doing stretching exercises and moving his mouth in silent prayer. I think he must not have been heard upstairs, because as soon as he comes out onstage in his black nylon muscle shirt and black stretch spandex bicycle shorts, the frat boys in the back row start their "WOOF WOOF WOOF WOOF WOOF" bit, and some guys back by the bar begin to boo before the music even starts.

But Manderson looks like a guy who isn't easily intimidated, and he takes a fierce stance onstage as if he's preparing to repel a human wave of Bruce Lee clones. When the band bangs into the hard funk beat of Tony Terry's "Lovey Dovey," Barry goes into a weight-lifter's squat, raises his arms over his head, and starts snapping his neck and jabbing the air with his elbows like a football linebacker practicing his forearm attack. On the downbeat, he springs up on the balls of his feet, grabs the microphone, and sings in a powerful but melodic voice that floats almost sweetly over the violent, driving beat. At the bridge he adds some heavy pelvic thrusting to his dance, and every female in the audience lets out a squeal. Suddenly, the entire theatre is on its feet, and both balconies have taken up the frat chant and made it a cheer: "WOOF WOOF WOOF WOOF WOOF WOOF WOOF." One woman in the front row is in ecstatic rapture, looking like she's about to clamor up on the stage and rip off Barry's spandex.

Even the German tourists are now with it, pumping their hands in the air and shouting, "JA—JA—JA—JA!"

Barry leaves the stage to thunderous applause and slumps against a light board, wrung out, exhausted, and beaming with pride.

I give the crowd a few minutes to settle down. But my doubts that the next highlight, Privacy, will be able to follow Barry are dispelled when the girls swing into their Stephanie Mills number. The crowd is back on its feet, and not even the guys at the bar boo or burp.

As the show goes on with each act bringing the audience to its feet, I realize how difficult it's going to be to choose the winner tonight. Bets are split backstage. Roger thinks the Big Guy's E.R.E. dance crew has the best shot. Lacey thinks Devora gave the best performance. Ralph II likes Privacy, but I think he might be smitten by one of the girls. Jackie thinks Fam-Lee. As for myself, after years of Amateur Nights, I know better than to make any predictions.

It doesn't much matter what I think, anyway, because it's not up to any of us backstage who wins tonight's three-thousand-dollar Super Dog prize money. We don't use any kind of applause meters or secret ballots or electronic listening devices. There are no judges with score cards, and there are no referees or special panels of experts to determine winners and losers. All judging is done by the audience. And they deliver their verdict by making as much noise as they can. The audience is the ultimate authority, the final arbiter. Their word is law—as it has been ever since I started Amateur Night.

The judging is simple. Ralph II handles the whole thing. As he announces each finalist, their supporters try to outscream and outholler the competition.

Holding a hand above pretty heads he'd like to know better, Ralph II says, "All right, folks—everyone who thinks Privacy is the winner, let 'em hear it!" A tidal wave could have rolled up from the ocean, sent breakers crashing into 125th Street, and you wouldn't know it for the noise Privacy's fans are making.

Once the applause subsides, Ralph II moves on to the next act. "This man came all the way from Tokyo to sing the blues the American way. Let's hear it for Yuki Ogiso!" If anyone ever told you that the Japanese are reserved, conservative, quiet, and hopelessly polite, bring 'em here tonight and see our Tokyo tourists making noise for their favorite rising son. They're joined by the Germans, who do some honest jumping and hollering of their own. All in all, it's a good showing for Yuki.

Now Ralph II steps behind Piscataway Pete. But too many great acts have come on since he opened the show, and Pete receives less applause than he got at the close of his number.

Barry Manderson always excites a crowd. Here he performs his song-and-dance number on the way to a second-place finish in our Super Top Dog, Amateur of the Year contest.

The balconies go wild for Trevor's E.R.E. dancers, and Devora wins sustained applause. But when Barry steps forward, I wish I had earplugs. The roar of approval is long and intense and seems to come from every corner of the theatre. I guess someone was listening to Barry's prayers after all.

There is just one group to go. But Fam-Lee was on relatively early in the program, and I assume that, like with Pete, the audience has forgotten how much they loved this act ninety minutes ago.

Now Ralph II raises his hand over the heads of the Goins Fam-Lee. But just as he does, little Brian darts from the pack. Then, in what is either a spontaneous burst of enthusiasm or an impossibly savvy move for a five-year-old, the little dynamo does an impromptu break dance, dropping to his knees, flipping over, and spinning in a circle on his back. It's like a little speed dance for joy, and the crowd roars approval.

Ralph II has to wait a full three minutes for the crowd to settle down. "Now," he says, "the brothers Goins, comin' to you from Plainfield, New Jersey, let's hear it for Tony, Berkley, Keith, Corey, and—" But no one hears Brian's name, because the crowd is on its feet and raising such a noise I start to think the 125th Street Fault is to blame.

Now Ralph II moves to the other end of the line and holds his hand above Privacy. The crowd is loud and enthusiastic. He next stands behind Barry and the roar begins again. But when he goes back to the Goinses, the response is positively seismic, and Ralph II declares Fam-Lee the top amateur winners of the year.

I'm happy to sign over the first-place prize money to Debra and her boys. But the real payoff for the Goinses comes down in the Green Room, after the show. That's when Jam Master Jay greets the boys with an offer they can't refuse. Before the group leaves the theatre, they accept the deal from Jam Master Jay to record and produce Fam-Lee's first album.

It's a dream come true for the Goins boys. Similar dreams have been coming true on our stage for the past half-century. And there is no reason such dreams won't continue to be realized in the next millennium—or at least until 2010, when the Big One finally brings the house down.

In 1983 my good friend, Percy Sutton, Chairman of Inner City Broadcasting, reopened the Apollo Theatre and the amateur night announcement once again burned the kilowatts on the Apollo marquee to the excitement and delightment of the Harlem community. Thus far there are two exceptional talents that we can brag about. And boy, do we love to brag about our future stars.

David Peaston won every plateau of the Amateur Night format for one year including the Super Dog, which pits the year's top winners against each other to determine the Amateur of the Year. David, by a landslide, was our 1986 winner and is now enjoying the status accorded today's top recording stars: his album has taken off and that's what artists pray for.

Maurice Star, record producer, writer, and manager, had been working with a new group of youngsters in Boston, Massachusetts, that he was really high on. Maurice was responsible for the act New

Edition. So when he wanted this new act to appear on the Amateur Night as guests for the exposure, that was good enough for me. During their introduction I really made a fuss about them, then said, "Ladies and gentlemen, meet the New Kids on the Block," and it was a wild and sensational meeting. They were positively great.

Today they are everybody's top chart favorite and it's nice to know they have not forgotten the Apollo audience or my personal pep speech. No drugs—just hugs—togetherness—hard work and dedication.

2

A New Era Begins

★ ★

Civilization began, they say, in its Mesopotamian cradle. Democracy developed in ancient Greece. And great entertainment was born in Harlem.

Harlem is where everything cool in our culture first got hot. The music, the dances, the lingo, the styles, and even the attitudes that have defined eras in popular American life—from jazz to bebop; from rhythm and blues to rock 'n roll, soul, funk, and rap; from the Charleston to the Lindy, Trucking and the Susie Q to the Jitterbug, the Twist, and today's Da Butt, Worm, and street dancing—all took root and blossomed in Harlem, sweet Harlem, the black capital with the Dutch name, the cradle from which America's liveliest arts and swingingest civilization sprang.

In the beginning of the twentieth century, African-Americans were virtually pouring into Harlem, with the greater portion of the migration coming up from the South. Many Southerners, thirty-five years after the Emancipation Proclamation, determined that going north was the correct route to Harlem and absolute freedom.

Back in the third decade of this century, a few years before I introduced Amateur Night at the Apollo Theatre and so transformed an old Irish burlesque hall into the world's most famous black entertainment showcase, something began cooking up in Harlem—the Jazz Age. And it soon had all America roaring. A new age of excitement was on the threshold.

In those days, Harlem was a many-splendored place. Its avenues and streets from 110th Street north were tree-laden. Seventh Avenue, now known as Adam Clayton Powell, Jr. Boulevard, was indeed at that time a beautiful boulevard. Sundays, when the Harlem churches turned out, Seventh Avenue became a sun-drenched fashion row where the beautiful people strolled, socialized, and displayed their finery. Actually no one would ever be caught any time on Seventh Avenue unless they were sartorially and tonsorially refined.

The Lafayette Theatre located between 131st and 132nd streets on Seventh Avenue was then Harlem's glamour venue and the camping ground for the great mix to gather and exchange all the dirt. Standing tall between the Lafayette Theatre and Connie's Inn was the Tree of Hope, believed by the black performers to be a fountainhead of good luck to those who were covered by its huge extended branches. While this belief was a myth the location was always star studded and attracted people hoping to see their favorites.

The double-decker open buses that traveled Seventh Avenue were Sunday's most delightful and affordable ride. You could cuddle up with your lady all the way down to Washington Square, approximately six miles away. Are you ready—the cost? Just one buffalo, a nickel. And if you owned wheels it was picture card beauty to drive through the magnificence of Central Park and exit at 110th Street and Seventh Avenue onto the boulevard of dreams and beauty.

Many of the strollers would stop at the Grey Shop, an eatery established by black entrepreneurs located on Seventh Avenue between 132nd and 133rd streets, for ham, spaghetti, and potato salad, an odd combination with a great taste. Others stopped at the Sugar Bowl located on Seventh Avenue at 137th Street for old-fashioned ice cream delights, while others preferred Bar-B-Que, soul, or Chinese. Then, of course, there were those who preferred dropping through the side entrance of the Big Apple, with their ladies. (This was, of course, prior to the lib movement and women's rights.) A bar and grill located on the northwest corner of 135th Street and Seventh Avenue, the Big Apple's name came from Harlem slang, meaning when you arrived in Harlem you were in the Big Apple, "God's Country." It's interesting to note that New York City in later years adopted it as its official nickname, "The Big Apple" with its meaningful definition "God's Country."

Strivers' Row residents, from 138th to 139th streets between Seventh and Eighth avenues, bragged about, and rightfully so, to having the most beautiful brownstone and limestone private houses in New York. Then there was Sugar Hill, a haven for those who could afford fireplaces, five bedrooms, penthouses, elevator accommodations, doormen, and a host of other amenities. Sugar Hill, from 145th Street to 160th Street, from Convent to Edgecombe avenues, was like a gorgeous mirage that really was.

Harlem was comprised of a community of God-fearing people working hard to accomplish a good life and educate their children. Then, as the twentieth century was taking shape, the do-gooders started loudly advocating Prohibition based on the proposition that drinking booze was an evil the country ought not to succumb to. They demanded booze be abolished. They predicted that eventually the younger generation would be consistently wetting its whistle, not to mention the ladies who would take up the not-so-ladylike excessive elbow bending. Then what would happen to the country. Their persistence and big mouths won the argument. Prohibition was legislated and rumor has it the fish partied for six months on the booze poured down the drain. Conversely, at about this time in the early 1920s, a new industry surfaced; the term was bootlegging. And a new group of suave businessmen emerged who syndicated their wares throughout the country on a sort of buy-or-die basis. Thus was born an era that made Harlem more exciting than the Boston Tea Party, Custer's Last Stand, or the St. Valentine Day Massacre.

It was dubbed the "Roarin' Twenties." Harlem nurtured, condoned, and embellished this flamboyant era that captured the imagination and triggered the excitement of people all over the world. As for the Harlem nightlifers, it opened the floodgate of new money that poured into Harlem like sweet syrup from a maple tree.

Harlem's nightclubs and after-hour joints were indeed the hallmark of its excitement, the beacon that illuminated the era. It was a chapter in American history that electrified the world with romanticized tales of mad dog killers, gorgeous whores, freaked-out hoodlums, and celebrated pimps and hustlers. At the same time, the era saw the fitful beginning integration, the rise and struggle of blacks, and the slowly emerging awareness of black politics.

Blacks, generally, considered Harlem their capital. It was the land of milk, honey, and money, and already the lure of its renaissance had captured the imagination of black artists, writers, musicians, and talented performing artists who brought their creativity to Harlem. It was the place where one could walk down the golden road to success.

And indeed a great many individuals representing all phases of the arts did reach the pinnacle of success and entrenched themselves in the archives of fame. Richard Wright, Langston Hughes, Romare Bearden, Duke Ellington, Fats Waller and Count Basie, to name a few. At that time, Harlem was far from being a ghetto, rather it was more like a paradise, as cosmopolitan as the left bank of Paris.

Harlem's glamorous nightlife became the place to go for Park Avenue socialites, Fifth Avenue's carriage trade, and Broadway's first nighters. It offered a daring and exciting panorama of events that were wild and mind-boggling. Harlem was on a roll; the numbers were jumping, the skin games were insane, and the house rent parties were funky, finger poppin' sessions featuring giants of the 88s, Fats Waller, Jimmy Johnson, Jellyroll Morton, among others. When they started foot stomping the blues and singing their wild double entendre numbers those packed railroad apartments went wild. The grease was popping, the chicken frying, the chitterlings doused and smothered with down home hot sauce and the taste buds cooled down with homemade bathtub gin. By now you were ten feet tall, slow dragging with the broads, backed up and rubbing the paint off the walls. The perfumed bodies were glistening from sweat under soft lights and the guys licking the drippings like a bear after honey. This was a house rent party, a Harlem special, with two objectives: make the rent money, and let the good times roll!

Then there was the thrill and excitement of women in Harlem's nightlife in clubs that presented an assortment of black charm with sensuous beauty and highly desired sweet-smelling bodies that would have caused Anthony to roll Cleopatra back up into the rug and return her down the Nile. This was the era that introduced Harlem's infamous machine gun violence, bathtub booze, crime syndicates, Prohibition, black music, and the epitome of black talent.

This was the Harlem to which came movie stars, royalty, politicians, VIPs and the hoi polloi in their chauffeur-driven shiny cars to carouse the night away. And wide-eyed visitors whose pulse would beat that extra four to the bar as they crossed 110th Street and Seventh Avenue and entered the city within a city. The Casbah of the world.

In the 1920s and '30s, Harlem was regarded by blacks as the center of the universe, the most exciting city on earth. That was during the period known as the Harlem Renaissance, when black writers, painters, poets, dancers, musicians, and playwrights made their presence felt in American cultural life with a creative outpouring unmatched before or since. It was a time when, as Langston Hughes said, "Harlem was in vogue." The brush artist Romare Bearden said this: "there were only two towns in all the world for the young, creative and daring black artist: You'd want to be either in Harlem then or in Paris."

There was a time when Harlem was nine miles and a day's ride to the city as indicated by a sign in front of an old wooden house still standing on 152nd Street between Amsterdam and Convent avenues. The rusty old sign survives and points the way to the once distant metropolis 9 MILES TO THE CITY. Nearby there is a famous cemetery, the Trinity, which runs from Amsterdam to Riverside Drive at 155th Street. There are soldiers from the Revolutionary War buried in there. The cannon George Washington placed to protect his Harlem headquarters during the revolution still stands sentry at the Jumel Mansion, 165th Street between Jumel Place and Edgecombe Avenue. Also in that part of Harlem named for the general, Washington Heights, is the spot where Aaron Burr was shot and killed in the duel with Alexander Hamilton, whose Harlem home, a historical landmark, still stands at 141st Street and Convent Avenue. So you see, Harlem has a history as long and exciting as America's own.

Before Harlem opened up to black families, most lived downtown, in the West Twenties, Forties, and Sixties, where from 61st street to 64th from Tenth to Eleventh avenues the neighborhood was known as the Jungle, where I grew up. Many great musicians came out of the Jungle, including Benny Carter, Freddy Jenkins, and Thelonious Monk.

Around the turn of the century, a real estate boom went bust. Developers had spent millions building a silver city for Manhattan's rich only to find they had created an ornate and enormous ghost town.

The wealthy families for whom uptown's lovely tree-lined boulevards and elegant brownstones had been designed were not eager to move from their current neighborhoods or to take the long elevated subway ride from the commercial districts downtown. For the next twenty years blacks began to move uptown to Harlem.

By the end of World War I, mass migrations of southern blacks from Jim Crow's Dixie had made Harlem the largest black city in America. By 1920, more blacks lived in Harlem than in any other area of New York, and the black city within the great metropolis was the Mecca of black America, a beacon for a people keen on inventing an American dream of their own.

Harlem was the Promised Land. Black people all over the country dreamed of living here. They arrived in New York by the hundreds, day after day, and made their way uptown. They could ride the subway for a nickel. Or they could catch a ferry in New Jersey to the busy docks at the foot of 125th Street. Ferries used to be the main mode of transportation across the Hudson River, where newcomers looked on in amazement as kids in kayaks surfed on the waves of the Weehawken or Fort Lee ferries.

Harlem was the place to be because it was the one place in the whole country where black men and women could express themselves and do their thing. Black talent and black culture could flourish in Harlem like nowhere else in the land. Harlem music, dance, and even language helped turn American culture black. Black musicians invented jazz, swing, rock and roll and bebop, and hip hop. Black dancers invented the Shimmy, Charleston, the Lindy Hop, the Black Bottom, Shorty George, Peckin, Susie Q and the Jitterbug. Black jive talk gave America "the Big Apple," "hippies," "groovy threads," "dime bags," "roaches," and "joints" thirty years before the sixties' counterculture adopted them as their own. The word "jazz" was jive for good lovin' in the 1800s, long before it came to denote the black sound that is now recognized as America's greatest contribution to world culture. Downtown folks "made beautiful music together," while uptown, we were making enormous jazz statements.

For millions of people, Harlem was an oasis of sanity in an insane world. And Harlem was beautiful to boot. Nobody thought of it as a ghetto. It was where people wanted to be, not where people wanted to escape from.

★   ★   ★

During the creative flowering known as the Harlem Renaissance, the Lincoln Theatre, where black performers from the TOBA circuit played to black audiences, was one of the two most important stages in Harlem. The other, the Lafayette (considered the premier revue), would later lose its management's battle to put the Apollo (the new kid on the block) out of business.

Seventh Avenue was the main artery where excitement, entertainment, and dreams flourished. The avenue was lined on both sides with shade trees and with traffic islands full of shrubbery and flowering gardens, the boulevard ran from the town houses of the black aristocracy living in splendor on the northern "Golden Edge" of Central Park all the way north to 155th Street at Washington Heights and Sugar Hill, where the stately homes that once housed Harlem's most famous citizens still stand, overlooking neighborhoods where the "Sugar Hill Gang" helped develop rap music in the late 1970s and early '80s.

At 125th Street, Seventh Avenue hit a strange anomaly—a segregated, all-white neighborhood in the heart of Harlem, where storekeepers and hotel, restaurant, and theatre owners practiced a form of segregation almost as strangling as South Africa's apartheid or our own Dixie's Jim Crow, the system of segregation that made racist crimes against blacks the law of the land. Today 125th Street is renowned as Harlem's Main Street. But at the height of Harlem development, 125th Street was a shopping center for the mostly Irish residents of neighborhoods surrounding Columbia University, Barnard College, and City College. It was "segregation without the signs." The only difference between 125th Street and Peachtree Street in Atlanta, Georgia, in those days was that in Harlem, the drinking fountains didn't say COLOREDS ONLY or WHITES ONLY.

Even the Harlem Chamber of Commerce was an all-white institution. In later years it was controlled by the Apollo's Frank Schiffman, along with Jack Blumstein, who owned Blumstein's, Harlem's department store across the street from the Apollo. For years, the chamber blocked blacks from leasing any store on the 125th Street artery. Black salespeople, store managers, and buyers were unheard of. Movie theatres bent over backwards to accommodate blacks—in the upper balcony. Harlem's famous Hotel Theresa was always fully booked—unless a customer was white, in which case a vacancy was miraculously discovered.

In those days, if you wanted to satisfy the hunger pangs on 125th Street, you inevitably came face to face with a maître d' who would have just one tiny table available, next to the toilet or right off the kitchen, making a pleasurable dining experience impossible. Frank's Restaurant on 125th Street near Eighth Avenue used to be one of the best in all the city. It was white all the way through. Frank's outdid the Cotton Club, where the kitchen was Chinese and the entertainment was black. But at Frank's, the kitchen was white, the cooks were white, the dishwashers, porters, waiters, and maître d's were white. Eventually it became integrated, although today, ironically, Frank's is a fish joint owned by Koreans.

Child's was another famous Harlem restaurant where no blacks were served before their time, which to management's mind would not arrive for many, many years.

The future site of the Apollo Theatre, at 253 West 125th Street, was occupied at the time by Hurtig & Seamon's Burlesque Theatre. There white men watched white women strip down to flesh-colored body stockings. The theatre itself was built as an Irish music hall in 1913. Hurtig took over in 1919 and made it a prime stop on the burlesque circuit for Fannie Brice and other stars. Segregated as any theatre down South, Hurtig & Seamon's never would have made it as a black theatre anyway. Black folks just didn't find strippin' a fittin' entertainment.

Near Hurtig & Seamon's was another, much smaller, whites-only burlesque house, called the Apollo Theatre, which was named for the Greek god of music and poetry but was operated by the maestro of burlesque, Herbert Minsky. In 1932, spearheaded by the great reformer, then Congressman Fiorello La Guardia, New York's burlesque houses were ordered closed, and both Hurtig's and the Apollo went dark. When Hurtig's reopened under Sidney Cohen's new ownership and management two years later, in January 1934, as the first theatre offering live entertainment for black audiences on 125th Street, it took the name of the smaller theatre down the street and became the 125th Street Apollo Theatre.

But the burlesque houses weren't the only theatres on 125th Street that catered to whites only. The Loews Victoria movie house was a lovely old show palace next door to Hurtig's; and whenever blacks entered, they were politely escorted up the broad and beautiful old marble staircases to the upper balconies, which were commonly called "nigger heaven." This was of course the source of a deep bitterness among the black people of Harlem. It was a bitterness and anger that would not be relieved until the civil disturbances of the mid-thirties when the black community finally said "Enough!"

★ ★ ★

At the corner of 124th Street and Lenox Avenue stood the headquarters of the Kingdom of Father Divine, who was one of the richest, most successful, and flamboyant religious leaders of the twentieth century. A spiritual despot who was revered by his followers as "God," Father Divine did much to relieve the suffering of Harlem's poorest—and in so doing managed to become one of the richest black men of his day.

Lots of fun was made of him, but Father Divine (whose real name was George Baker) did good things for the poor. They could find work at one of his "peace" shoe-shine stands or one of his other employment centers. Also, one could eat at a Father Divine hot food place for fifteen cents, or for free if they had nothing.

As charismatic as any modern evangelist or cult leader, Father Divine invited followers to live in church-owned dormitories in which men and women were housed separately, regardless of their marital status. Anyone moving into the Kingdom turned over all possessions to him.

Hordes of people worshiped Father Divine. He had a big, chauffeur-driven car with a throne mounted in back. He would draw crowds wherever he went. The sudden appearance of Muhammad Ali, Michael Jackson, and Bill Cosby all together at the same time *might* generate the kind of excitement that Father Divine inspired. Crowds gathered wherever he appeared. When his car turned the corner, there was always a mad rush. His people revered him. One of their slogans about him was that "the world is in his jug and the stopper is in his hand."

But Father Divine's excesses and enormous personal wealth made skeptics of many would-be supporters. His church of "Righteous Government" was weakened when the Father, who advocated chastity for his followers, married a beautiful young white follower in a lavish wedding ceremony. The press made a scandal out of the wedding. But Father Divine's flock did not break ranks. He was "God," and she was "Angel." His followers managed to work it all out biblically.

But by the 1940s, Father Divine had become an object of investigation. During World War II, hounded by questions about his finances, he left Harlem and relocated his headquarters in Philadelphia.

On Seventh Avenue at 131st Street, the very heart of Harlem's Jazz Age, there stood the famed Lafayette Theatre, where many great black stars trod the boards. (It was also a place where I began to develop my craft as a young hoofer who would go on to become a bandleader, actor, producer, comedy writer, and master of ceremonies.)

Before the Apollo took the title, the Lafayette was the premier showcase for black talent in America. Its marquee illuminated the night sky over Seventh Avenue, advertising show times and prices, circa 1930—ten cents for the ten a.m. show, twenty cents for the matinee, and a hefty forty cents if you wanted an orchestra seat at night. The Lafayette, which was the flagship of the Round the World circuit, the big time for black vaudeville, was owned by Leo Brecker and managed by his hatchet man, Frank Schiffman. Schiffman was a smart businessman. But he was also a ruthless competitor who would do anything, including take advantage of his black employees and exploit the great black artists who worked for him, in order to increase his profits and beat down the opposition. Schiffman had a list in his office of all the performers who had offended him and were not allowed to play the Lafayette. My former dance partner, Eddie Rector, signed one of Schiffman's contracts for one price, and when Schiffman paid him a lesser amount, Eddie flew into a rage. Eddie went home and got himself a pistol and told Schiffman he better honor that contract or he was going to ventilate him. Schiffman hid in his office and called the cops, who hauled Eddie off to jail. Schiffman prosecuted Eddie for threatening him. I know a lot of performers who wished Eddie had pulled that trigger.

Several knuckleheaded writers of Harlem show business have glorified Schiffman as a great showman. Believe me, this he was not. He was one of the many self-ordained great white fathers of Harlem. Schiffman and other theatrical managers ran their theatres like small plantations where they were powerful masters of all they surveyed. One of Schiffman's cronies, a talent manager named Nat Nazarro, had an exclusive roster of leading black acts who could not make a move without his okay. Nazarro had some top, top talent under his thumb, including such great comedy duos as Moke and Poke, Chuck and Chuckles, and Cook and Brown. But of all Nazarro's rip-offs, his crowning glory was to sign Buck and Bubbles to a contract for life—with an option for renewal.

After the Apollo took over as the premier black theatre in Harlem, Schiffman's Lafayette went under and later became the home of

This photo from the Schomburg Collection is believed to have been taken inside Connie's Inn, which stood at the corner of 131st Street and Seventh Avenue. The club was immortalized in *Connie's Hot Chocolates*, the Fats Waller-Andy Razaf musical that enjoys revivals to this day. On the sidewalk out front stood one of Harlem's most famous show-biz landmarks—the Tree of Hope.

the New Deal's Federal Negro Theatre, where Orson Welles and John Houseman produced *Native Son*, starring Canada Lee, and the first-ever all-black production of *Macbeth*.

Next door to the Lafayette was one of the outstanding clubs in all Harlem. Connie's Inn, along with the Cotton Club and Small's Paradise, was one of Harlem's big three hot spots where the black musical explosion was centered. Connie's was owned by Connie Immerman and his brother George, white men who used to own a deli in an old black neighborhood downtown. Connie used to have a delivery boy working for him named Fats Waller, who would become world famous as the great stride piano player and composer of such classics as "Honeysuckle Rose," "Jitterbug Waltz," and "Ain't Misbehavin'."

Connie's presented a lot of great talent. The Mills Brothers, the great dance team of Meers and Meers, Snakehip Tucker, and Peg Leg Bates all came out of Connie's, where they installed an organ specially built for Fats Waller. Fats and his lyricist Andy Razaf scored the Broadway musical success "Connie's Hot Chocolates." Razaf was a prolific lyricist who wrote more than five hundred songs, including the lyrics to such Waller compositions as "What Did I Do to Be So Black and Blue," "Sposin," and "Honeysuckle Rose." Because of his name many people thought he was a white man, but he was the son of a Malagasy nobleman. He also collaborated with Eubie Blake and W.C. Handy. I think he died in 1973.

The corner in front of Connie's was a show-business hangout shaded by the Tree of Hope, another famous Harlem landmark. The tall chestnut tree would later play a significant role in the history of the Apollo Theatre, but only after it was ripped up by the roots and sold off as firewood.

Just two blocks north of Connie's Inn, on 133rd Street, the hottest all-night spots in all Manhattan roared Prohibition away. Known around town as "Swing Street" years before Fifty-second Street downtown took the name, 133rd was like Sodom and Gomorrah by gaslight, by far the most exciting street in all New York City and perhaps the world at that time. Lights didn't go on along that wild block until three in the morning. It would be pitch dark and quiet at midnight, but by three o'clock the street would be choked with traffic. You couldn't move on the sidewalks they were so crowded, and chauffeur-driven luxury cars lined the block, which was lit up like New Orleans at Mardi Gras time. There were fifteen or twenty places jumpin' at full voltage all through the wee small hours of the morning.

Spawned by passage of the Volstead Act in 1919, and nurtured by Prohibition until its end in 1933, speakeasies catering to integrated "black and tan" audiences thrived on 133rd Street and attracted visitors from around the world as well as the rich and famous gangsters,

The Nest Club was one of the great 133rd Street after-hours speakeasies that flourished in Harlem during Prohibition.

musicians, and celebrities of the day. Clubs with names like the Nest, the Madhouse, the Chicken Shack, Pod's and Jerry's, and Mexico's became famous throughout the jazz-loving world. So flagrant were the speakeasies and booze-peddling after-hour joints that New York's Finest worked as bouncers and security guards for club owners who sold high-priced, watered-down illegal booze by the bucketful.

People could see things on 133rd Street they didn't see anywhere else in the city. The Madhouse had a singer who specialized in bawdy songs. That wasn't so unusual, but the singer was really a woman who dressed like a man—Gladys Bentley. The scene lasted until eight or nine in the morning, and it was always a sight during the morning rush hour when all the carriage trade in evening clothes would be out on the curb looking for their limos while all the poor working stiffs headed underground to board the "iron horse."

That was Harlem's high life on 133rd Street. But for a real swingin' low-down time, there was an even deeper underground scene happening in Harlem. Fats Waller made the Harlem rent parties world famous in his song "The Joint Is Jumpin'." Just about any night of the week, someone who was having trouble coming up with the landlord's money would cook up a barrel of chitterlings, fry up a mess of greasy, finger-lickin' chicken, roll up the rug, wheel in a piano, and have a funky, get-down house rent party. They'd invite all their friends and put the word out on the street that there would be eating and dancing and drinking till dawn. Everybody for blocks around would make the scene, and they'd party until the cows came home. The host would provide the music and shelter, and the guests would pay for all the food and drink they could get down. Folks would get to dancin' and lovemakin' right there in the living room. A couple might start doing the Lindy, and all the boys would gather round to watch those loose skirts fly. And lots of times women would wear nothing but dark skin underneath, since they didn't have Danskin in those days.

The Boulevard of Dreams passes Paradise—Ed Small's Paradise—a couple of blocks north of 133rd Street, at 2294 Seventh Avenue at 135th Street. Small's was made famous as the Black Venus Club in Carl Van Vechten's best-selling Jazz Age novel, *Nigger Heaven*. One of the great black clubs of the twenties, Small's was renowned for its dancing waiters, who would do the Charleston and splits and tap dance while balancing glasses full of bootlegged drinks on their trays. Small's was one of the few uptown nightclubs owned by blacks. Ed Small used to run an elevator before he became host of one of the great clubs of the day.

Another famous entrepreneur lived near Small's Paradise in an enormous mansion on 136th Street between Seventh and Lenox Avenues. Madame C. J. Walker, the hair-straightening mogul, was the richest person in Harlem. Madame Walker grew up poor as you can be and still stay alive. Her parents were both born into slavery. They died when C. J. was seven. She lived in orphanages until she was fourteen, when she got married. She was a widow at twenty, broke and alone. When she died, she was the richest self-made woman in America, black or white. Madame Walker's product straightened kinky hair. It sold so well—everybody in Harlem and in black communities across the country bought it—that she became a millionaire many times over.

A generous and progressive lady who gave away millions to help the poor, Madame Walker moved up to an estate on the Hudson. But her daughter, A'Lelia, stayed on in the mansion in Harlem and became famous for her outrageous parties. Huge affairs that lasted days on end, A'Lelia's extravaganzas made the Great Gatsby's look like tea parties. She had orchestras and tables full of food and ice sculptures and fountains that pumped champagne. The famous party scene in Van Vechten's novel was based on a little soirée at A'Lelia's that lasted for four weeks.

If Seventh Avenue could talk, it would keep quiet around 138th Street, where the moral heart of Harlem resides in the Abyssinian Baptist Church. In the 1920s, the Reverend Adam Clayton Powell, Sr., was pastor. His son, the future congressman, grew up in the church, along with the son of an assistant minister, Thomas Waller, nicknamed Fats. When Adam, Jr., eulogized Fats Waller in 1943, he spoke of sneaking into the church, then located on 53rd Street, with Fats, whose feet were too short to reach the organ pedals—so Adam pumped while Fats played. "Music just poured out of him," Adam said. "And he didn't play hymns."

From the Abyssinian, the Boulevard of Dreams crosses "Strivers' Row," the name locals gave West 138th and 139th streets, where the spreading shade trees and elegant brownstones and town houses designed by Stanford White represented the economic Shangri-la many strived for. Going east one block to Lenox Avenue, at the corner of 140th Street, stood a building that should have been enshrined as an American cultural landmark. A nondescript, low-rise row of brick buildings occupies the site now. But a lifetime ago, it was home to the greatest dance hall of all, the home of happy feet, the Savoy Ballroom.

When the Savoy first opened, it was a dance hall featuring dime-a-dance taxi dancing. Then the advent of the big bands changed the policy. You could still dance, but you'd get slapped in the face or worse if you offered a dime to some beautiful lady for a sprint around that magnificent dance floor.

The Savoy, which was owned by Moe Gale and operated by Charles Buchanan, covered an entire block, from 140th to 141st Street. The enormous second-floor ballroom was flanked by two wide, stately staircases that swept up from the street. It was a true dance palace, elaborately done up with chandeliers, brilliant murals, carpeted floors, and booths for drinking and people-watching. Heeding a strict semi-formal dress code, patrons always dressed to the hilt. But many couldn't hold a candle to the Savoy bouncers, who had to be the most efficient and best dressed in the business. Big, musclebound bruisers in tuxedos, they were also very smooth and gentlemanly. If a skirmish broke out on the dance floor, the courtly hulks would descend on the brawlers in an instant. The bouncers would lift the poor fools over their heads and carry them kicking and squirming across the ballroom floor, down the stairs and out the door, where they'd be unceremoniously deposited onto the sidewalk along with tomorrow's trash.

The Savoy became a proving ground for dance crazes destined to sweep the country, especially the Lindy Hop developed by the Savoy's regulars, whose frenzied, near-acrobatic skills were legend. Every night the dancers were egged on to new heights of daring and abandon by the great dance bands of the day.

The Charleston, one of the biggest dance fads ever to sweep the globe, was being done in Harlem before it was banned in Boston. People think the Charleston was invented by F. Scott Fitzgerald or some other famous Jazz Age personality. But the step actually evolved in Harlem, then exploded when Fats Waller's stride piano mentor, Jimmy Johnson, of New Brunswick, New Jersey, wrote a song called "Charleston." It had the perfect *bop-bop bop-bop* beat to go with the new dance step: "Charles-ton, Charles-ton made in Carolina." So the dance got its name from Jimmy's song.

Even more exciting than the Charleston was the wildly frenetic Lindy Hop. The Lindy (named for Charles Lindbergh's "hop" across the ocean in 1927) was a tremendously exciting dance, the most fantastic of all those born in Harlem. Rocking on the beat, dancers threw their partners high over their heads. They swung them and spun them, twisted and twirled them in a blur of motion and wild abandon. The women would hop on their heels and jump up and wrap their legs around their partners' waists. (The jitterbug, which became popular much later, is a drastically toned-down version of the Lindy.)

The Lindy made the Savoy Ballroom world famous; tourists poured into the Savoy by the busload to see this outrageous dance. The Savoy's best dancers were organized into a professional team known as Whitey's Lindy Hoppers. But in the forties, Whitey's crack dance group included one pair of dancers who were more amazing than all the rest—and none of Whitey's dancers were slouches. Whitey's star was over seven feet tall. He must have worn size 24 or 25 shoes—he would have been great for the Knicks. He was tall as a house, and his partner was a tiny little thing, no more than five feet tall. And could both of them dance! Needless to say, it was an amazing sight to see those two fly around the dance floor like high-speed ballet stars. Every year when the *Daily News* held its Harvest Moon Ball, Tall and Small would win the Lindy contest in a high-speed walk.

The Savoy was basically a black ballroom popular among whites, who were welcome and made to feel comfortable by management and regular customers alike. But two blocks north and a world away from the Savoy, at the corner of 142nd Street and Lenox Avenue, was the most famous nightclub in America: the Cotton Club. It was also one of the great oddities of American life—a nightclub in the heart of Harlem owned and operated by white gangsters who hired black talent to entertain whites-only audiences. Strict rules forbade service or even entrance to black customers. Duke Ellington could play the Cotton Club and broadcast his radio show live from the Cotton Club. But Duke Ellington couldn't sit and have a drink at the Cotton Club.

Racist and unjust as they were, these perverse segregationist policies were protested only halfheartedly, if at all, by human-rights advocates. The fact is, the Cotton Club did not embitter the black community because there was 100 percent black employment in the club. The entertainment and the help were all black, except in the kitchen, where it was all Chinese. The greatest black musicians, dancers, and producers did some of the best work of their lives at the Cotton Club, making it a haven for black entertainers who otherwise might never have been seen by a white audience. But most important, the club lured the carriage trade to Harlem, where entertainment was the main legal industry. It brought money to Harlem that would not have been there otherwise.

Opened as the Douglas Casino, a club offering motion pictures

COTTON CLUB PARADE

on the ground floor and dancing on the second, the venue was purchased in 1920 by black heavyweight boxing champion Jack Johnson, who sold it three years later to Owney Madden, a former Hell's Kitchen street-gang leader. Madden and his crew turned the Cotton Club into a gangsters' lair, a gangland flagship that became the New York underworld's favorite hangout. During the 1920s and '30s, the city's most notorious hoodlums included Dutch Schultz and Legs Diamond. The bad boys of the era, they were treated like celebrities. Everyone knew what they looked like—they read about them in books, magazines, and newspapers, saw them in newsreels and in movies. Hoods were an attraction almost as powerful as the Cotton Club's music. The club made Owney so rich and respectable that his own illegal hooch—Madden's No. 1—became one of the best-sellers in the Prohibition era.

When the Cotton Club opened for business in the fall of 1923 with seating for seven hundred and a "jungle" decor featuring loads of bamboo, palm trees, and exotic animal skins, the manager was Madden's second-in-command, George "Big Frenchie" DeMange. Frenchie was a racist thug with a nasty and perverse violent streak who made no secret of his contempt for blacks. Frenchie enforced the club's admissions policies and was responsible for some strange house rules. It was Frenchie who insisted the Cotton Club's gorgeous chorus girls all have light, "high yaller" skin tone, stand over five feet six inches, and be under twenty-two years of age. Those "high yallers" in the chorus line were a major club attraction. There was one exceptionally beautiful girl named Amy Spencer who had flaming red hair and green eyes. Another gorgeous dancer, named Marion Egbert, had natural blond hair and luminous blue eyes.

The Cotton Club really began to make its name in 1927, when Madden hired a then little-known orchestra headed by a piano player named Duke Ellington. Duke's band had a commitment to play a date in Philadelphia when the Cotton Club gig was offered. Clarence Robinson, who would later work at both the Cotton Club and the Apollo Theatre, was producing at the Philadelphia theatre. Clarence refused to release Ellington's band from its contract until he received a sug-

(Opposite) The greatest night spot of them all, the Cotton Club, which stood at the corner of 142nd Street and Lenox Avenue, brought the carriage trade to Harlem. The Cotton Club's gorgeous "sepia" dancers were among the most beautiful women in the world.

The great palaces of Europe never produced royalty the equal of our Duke Ellington, who became world famous during his long tenure at the Cotton Club. In the 1930s, two of the leading lights of the classical music world, symphony conductor Leopold Stokowski and composer Dmitry Shostakovich, declared that the Duke was among the world's greatest living composers. Here he is shown during my Blue Ribbon Salute radio broadcast over WMCA in the 1950s.

gestion he couldn't ignore from Madden's associates: ''Be big,'' Clarence was told, ''or be dead.''

The Cotton Club made a number of talents famous, including Cab Calloway and the Nicholas Brothers, the Berry Brothers, and Ethel Waters, but it was Duke who made the Cotton Club. His Jungle Band, which took its name from the club decor, had a revolutionary sound and style. He had Johnny Hodges, one of the greatest alto sax players of all time, Lawrence Brown on trombone, Freddy Jenkins, Bubber Miley, Cootie Williams on trumpets, Sonny Greer on drums, and the great Ivie Anderson on vocals. Duke had so many wonderful people, any one of them could have been a bandleader in his own right.

Duke's music at the Cotton Club went out over the radio on NBC's "Caravan of Music" broadcasts. Duke was always great, and radio made him a national star. Later, when we needed to get the word out about the excitement of the Apollo's Amateur Night in Harlem show, I remembered what radio did for Duke. It was something I filed away and kept in the back of my mind.

So were the glory days of the Cotton Club. After Prohibition was repealed in December 1933, the bottom fell out of the market for illegal booze, and the white warlords who depended on it began to loosen their bloody grip on Harlem. In February 1936, the mob closed its flagship and moved the Cotton Club downtown.

Many talented people became stars at the Cotton Club. Cab Calloway's orchestra took over as the Cotton Club's featured band after the Duke went to Hollywood and toured. Still doing the hi-de-ho after all these years, Cab and I go way, way back.

Before concluding, we'll swing south to 116th Street, where the Italian mob had its headquarters. The mob first moved into Harlem when Dutch Schultz muscled in and took over the numbers racket from a Hispanic gangster named Pompeii. The "insurance business," which is what they called the numbers racket, was a big, big business. People played it like they play the lottery today. One popular game was based on a number hidden in a popular newspaper cartoon, a cartoon that still runs today, though without the daily number. I remember one week when a comedian, Clarence Foster, of the Foster and Joiner comedy team, hit the numbers three nights running. The games paid off six to one, and Clarence made close to $18,000 in three nights. Poor Clarence had a beat-up old car on which he owed $750. He could have bought himself a couple of brand-new Cadillacs with the money he scored on numbers. But less than three months later, the finance people came and took Clarence's car away for failure to make the payments.

A guy named Vincent "Mad Dog" Coll, who was the Crazy Joe Gallo of his day, tried to take on Schultz's mob after Schultz had a fatal argument with Coll's brother. On the warpath to avenge his brother's murder, Mad Dog walked into a cafeteria on Lenox Avenue near Schultz's office and opened up with a tommy gun on some of Schultz's boys. Later he shot up 107th Street. Tragically, a small child was shot and killed in the crossfire, and the newspapers dubbed Coll "the Mad Dog Killer." But Coll wasn't cowed. Instead of going into permanent hiding, he did something crazy. Some time earlier, Coll had kidnapped Connie Immerman and held him for ransom. He got away with it once, so he figured he'd try again. But this time, he made the mistake of kidnapping Owney Madden's right hand, Big Frenchie, and held him for a reputed $35,000 ransom.

Coll got the money, but he might as well have bought his death warrant with it. Soon after the Big Frenchie kidnapping, somebody made a deal with Coll's girlfriend. Two hoods were waiting when Coll walked into a Twenty-third Street drugstore to take a call from

(Opposite) The Plantation Club, located on 126th Street off Lenox Avenue, was famous for this mural, a collage of black show-business greats, including, as you can see, some fetching burlesque "artistes." The Plantation's owners made the mistake of competing with the Cotton Club. After the notorious bootlegger Owney Madden, who ran the Cotton Club, sent some of his henchmen to bust up the competition, the Plantation never regained popularity.

Eddie Rector and I were on the road constantly when I posed for this photo in 1931. In those days, smoking was the mark of a suave and debonair gentleman.

his best girl. Police said 123 slugs were fired at Coll as he stood in the phone booth, so tiny he couldn't get to his gun. The button men who did it were never caught. But everybody in Harlem knew one of them was the same guy who later killed Dutch Schultz himself. He also pulled off the most famous hit in New York history when he shot Albert Anastasia in his barber's chair.

When the Apollo Theatre broke the 125th Street color barrier and opened in January 1934, Prohibition and the little clubs it spawned were watered down. In the spring of the following year, on March 19, 1935, blacks smashed windows and looted stores on 125th Street in a spontaneous venting of lingering rage against segregation. The so-called riots helped end the grand illusion that Harlem was full of happy-go-lucky blacks too busy singin' and dancin' and struttin' to want a slice of the American pie.

The New York *Evening Journal,* a white daily, began an editorial campaign about the dangers Harlem posed to innocent white visitors. The paper created a terrible paranoia about Harlem. It was pictured as a jungle full of "headhunters" eager to butcher and devour any white person who dared stray Harlem way. Already beset by depressing economic conditions and mob wars over turf, the articles spread the belief among once adventurous whites that black anger equaled antiwhite hatred.

Yet in the midst of the ruins of the Harlem Renaissance, the seed for a new flowering of Harlem life was about to be planted. By the end of the year, Sid Cohen's Apollo Theatre introduced (Ralph Cooper's) Amateur Night in Harlem; and, if only for one night a week, Harlem was in vogue again.

3

Amateur Nights in Harlem, or How to Drown on Dry Land

★ ★

In the first weeks of 1934, a quarter-page ad appeared in Harlem newspapers and quickly became the talk of uptown. A MESSAGE TO HARLEM THEATRE-GOERS was presented as an open letter to readers.

"Dear Friends and Patrons," it began,

> The opening of the 125th Street Apollo Theatre next Friday night (January 26th), will mark a revolutionary step in the presentation of stage shows. The most lavish and colorful extravaganzas, produced under the expert direction of Clarence Robinson, internationally known creator of original revues, will be a weekly feature.
>
> The phrase, "the finest theatre in Harlem," can be aptly applied to this redecorated and refurbished temple of amusement.
>
> Courtesy and consideration will be the watchword of the management, truly a resort for the better people.
>
> High Fidelity RCA sound equipment, the same as used by Radio City Music Hall, and an innovation in public address systems, has been installed and we feel certain that the 125th Street Apollo Theatre will be an entertainment edifice that Harlem will take pride in showing off to neighboring communities.

For many folks, the first reaction to reading that ad was "Yeah, right!" That so-called entertainment edifice on 125th Street had been a segregated, whites-only showplace for more than twenty years. Everyone knew that the owners of Hurtig & Seamon's Burlesque Theatre were no fans of the tans. The policy at Hurtig's was the same as it was at Blumstein's Department Store across the street—No Coloreds Need Apply. Blacks didn't work behind the curtain or on the stage. And they certainly didn't rest their weary souls in the orchestra seats.

But most of Harlem's show people knew the code and got the ad's real message loud and clear. They understood that though for one reason or another the theatre's new management did not want to come right out and announce it, this new Apollo Theatre was about to become the first-ever theatre on 125th Street offering live entertainment by black artists for black audiences. That in itself was a "revolutionary" step indeed. And the irony of the ad's wording was not lost on those in the know. The real meaning Sid Cohen wanted to convey was clear. Hurtig's was a "temple of [prurient white] amusement" and it was about to be reborn as a "resort for the better [that is to say, black] people." Everyone uptown was further pleased to hear that the new theatre would be equipped with a sound system the equal of Radio City's, which meant it could be used to blow down the walls of segregation on 125th Street. And when that happened, all Harlem would definitely sit up and take notice. Euphemistic as the wording was, everyone in the business got the message the Apollo was putting out: "Black brothers and sisters, come on down!"

I read that ad and I thought, "About time." But that was as far as my interest went. I certainly had no intention of entering that theatre as anything more than a paying customer. Black Gotham already had a theatre, the Lafayette, where I was working as a performer and producer. The Lafayette Theatre was known throughout the country as the biggest, the best, and the most famous black vaudeville theatre there was.

While still in my teens, I had already worked the greatest theatres in show land, first as half of a "class act," high-style dance team with the great Eddie Rector, and later as a bandleader of the Kongo Knights Orchestra. I dug my steady gig at the Lafayette, where I was part of a peerless production team led by Clarence Robinson, who had come over to the Lafayette from the Cotton Club, where he produced and choreographed some of the club's most legendary revues.

Clarence and I developed shows that played the Lafayette for a week's run before going out on the Round the World circuit—black vaudeville's big time.

I worked in the most prestigious black theatre in America. It was a good gig at a glamourous theatre. It was the top. Any move from there would be down. So when Clarence told me he was talking to Morris Sussman about going to his new theatre on 125th Street, my first question was "Why? What for?" Clarence said Sussman and his boss, Sidney Cohen, a theatre owner who was in direct competition with the Lafayette's owner, Leo Brecker, were determined to make a go of this new venture, the 125th Street Apollo Theatre. "But they can't be serious," I said, "going up against the Lafayette—and on 125th Street yet!"

Clarence told me they were dead serious. Sussman, he said, had hosted a meeting at the Renaissance Casino with the top theatre critics in Harlem. He invited a dozen newspapermen to the meeting. Clarence said they must have gone through half a dozen bottles of scotch, rye, and bourbon. Sussman laid out his plans—"Colored shows for colored audiences."

According to Clarence, the news guys said that as much as they liked Sussman, he didn't have a prayer. Sussman was dreaming if he thought people would suddenly stop patronizing the Lafayette and start going all the way down to 125th Street. Blacks never were welcome on 125th, and never would be. Besides, they said, Harlem couldn't support another black vaudeville house. The Lafayette was king of the hill. Sussman and Cohen were just asking to get knocked on their butts.

"So why are you doing it?" I asked Clarence.

"Because Morris Sussman says he can do it and I believe him."

I thought Clarence was cracked. "You mean you're willing to quit a sure thing at the Lafayette, where you're top man, to go to a theatre the smart money says is a surefire failure?"

"He said something else, Coop," Clarence said. "He said I should think about going down there because 'it's the progressive thing to do.' Those were his words: 'It's the progressive thing.' "

Later, I would remember those words myself. But at the moment, I didn't think too much about it. I thought Clarence was making a questionable business decision. Whether or not it was socially progressive didn't seem to be of any real concern. Anyway, it never even occurred to me that *I* might sign up with Morris Sussman's new theatre too.

But then a funny thing happened. I ran into my boss, the Lafayette's general manager, Frank Schiffman, backstage at the theatre one night.

"Hey," I said, "did you hear about this new theatre, the Apollo? I guess it's going to open up down there on 125th Street. What do you think? Can they make a go of it?"

I thought Schiffman would be interested in talking about what was going on down on 125th Street. After all, he was in the business. But Schiffman didn't want to discuss it. He didn't even want to hear about it. Instead, he got all hot behind his collar. He spit out an ultimatum. "Anybody who jumps ship and goes to work for Morris Sussman at the Apollo Theatre is on my blacklist," he said. "That's the end of their career in show business. It's over. They will never work again—period. Tell 'em you heard it from me personally. Go tell 'em!"

I had to turn around and see who Schiffman was talking to. Maybe I'd walked into the middle of an argument. But there was nobody behind me. I didn't know if I should laugh out loud or sock him one right in the mouth. I couldn't imagine anyone in his right mind flying off the handle like that for no reason.

I realized Schiffman's problem was that he didn't want any opposition. As a theatre person, Frank Schiffman knew how to operate a theatre, but he didn't care about the community he operated it in. I realized right then and there that Schiffman didn't give a hang for the people who worked for him or for the performers who appeared in his theatre or even for the paying customers who were in his audience and who put the food on his dinner table up there in Westchester County, where he lived.

That was why Clarence Robinson took Sussman's offer. He knew that all Schiffman cared about was money. Doing the progressive thing was the last thing on his mind. But to go to work for a management team that was willing to pioneer black show business on 125th Street—*that* was something worth risking a career for. There was more meaning and more personal achievement in Sussman's venture than in all Frank Schiffman's balance sheets. Schiffman had no concern for the social progress that could be achieved by striking a blow against segregation on 125th Street. He was worried about a new competitor. He was afraid the Apollo might take dollars away from the Lafayette. He didn't care that the Apollo represented something good for the black community—namely, the beginning of the end of segregation on 125th Street.

So Schiffman threatened me. He said he would ruin my career. "I mean you too, Cooper," he said. "If I hear that you've even *talked* to Morris Sussman about his piece-of-crap theatre, you will be through. You won't work in Harlem—you won't work in Philadelphia or Washington or Baltimore. You won't work *anywhere!*" He went on and on. He said I would be washed up and forgotten if I dared to turn my back on him. Frank Schiffman really saw himself as the great white father of black show business. All his life that's how he saw himself—the great white father. "You go to work for the Apollo Theatre," he said, "and I will write your name at the top of my shit list."

Well, the minute I heard this, I knew it was "Apollo Theatre, here I come!" I had gone to work that night with a mild interest in the new theatre opening on 125th Street. But once I talked to Frank Schiffman and heard him say "Absolutely *no!*"—I just had to say "Absolutely *yes!*" Of course, more would be heard from Frank Schiffman—much more. But it was a wonderful feeling of liberation to tell him where he could shove his blacklist.

The difference between Morris Sussman and Frank Schiffman was simple: Sussman was a wonderful person. He was not acquainted with black show business at all; but he had the absolute willingness to learn and to do things that were right for the people who worked for him, for the performers, and for the black community itself. Sussman was smart and he was fair, and when he put out the word that he wanted to make the Apollo a stage for black entertainment, all theatre people hailed it as a breakthrough and a progressive step in the history of Harlem show business.

So word got out fast about the Apollo. Everyone in show business knew that this was where the action was—which is why from the very get-go we had a great stock company and crew. Clarence and I were able to bring a lot of people with us from the Lafayette; many of their best people were eager to leave. The Apollo's backstage was a completely different backstage than the Lafayette's, where people were extremely unhappy, mistreated, and mad.

There was a stage manager at the Lafayette who was like a CIA spy for Frank Schiffman. Anything you did, Sam Craig reported to Frank. Sam was a rat because Schiffman was always screaming at him. So Sam screamed back—but not at Schiffman. Sam was like the dog in the old story about the man who kicks the servant, who kicks the dog, which bites the guests. We could never figure out who was kicking Schiffman. But somebody must have been, because he was kicking hell out of poor Sam Craig, and Sam Craig liked to bite everybody in sight.

In the beginning, there was no kicking going on at the Apollo Theatre, so we were able to get all sorts of good people from theatres in Washington and Philadelphia as well as New York to come on board. The cast was tops. We had Clarence, who hired all the gorgeous dancers and did all the choreography with his fantastic chorus line. We had Jimmy Baskett, who was a great straight man, and an excellent talent who later played Uncle Remus in the Disney movie *Song of the South.* Vivian Harris and Adelaide Marshall were two great situation comediennes. We also had me—and I was willing to do everything, from production work and sketch and comedy writing to singing, dancing, comedy, and acting as master of ceremonies.

Right from the beginning, the crew was tops too. From day one, the Apollo had few sound or light problems, no technical glitches, fritzing microphones—none of that. Cues were always right on time. The sound was terrific. I brought in most of the people myself, including a stagehand from the Lafayette named Norman Miller who would become famous as our Amateur Night Executioner, Porto Rico. There was also Bob Hall, an ace electrician from the Howard Theatre in Washington, where I also got crack carpenters Stephen Miller and Phil Pearman. These guys were geniuses. They built sets at the Apollo that were just fantastic—ocean liners, circus trains, antebellum mansions, city street corners, courthouses. Anything you could imagine, these guys could create.

The crew rigged retracting microphones that rose right up from the basement (the space that is now the Green Room) and through the stage floor and slid back down when they weren't needed, so you didn't have stagehands running out to set mikes at every set change. They crafted a bandstand that rolled on tracks under the stage so the whole band could glide from the back of the stage right up to the lip. The audience thought the orchestra was going to float right offstage and land in their laps. It was fantastic.

The production number is from one of my pictures, *The Duke Is Tops*. The "Music Is Medicine" banner behind the bandstand really grabs me.

The Apollo opened with a staff, cast, and crew of eighty men and women. We all pulled together because we knew we were pioneers of a progressive movement in black theatre. It was an intoxicating feeling, but being the new kids on the block meant we really had to bend over backwards to make it a success. Everyone worked hard. Each morning I'd arrive by eleven a.m., and stay until two and sometimes three the next morning. The schedule was hell. We would be doing four shows a day, five on Sunday, seven days a week. That's twenty-nine shows (sometimes more) every week, all year long.

As it turned out, it never got easy. After every show, we'd come offstage and there was always someone yelling "Half-hour! Half-hour!" That meant there was just half an hour before the next show started. In that time they'd turn out the crowd and bring in another, while backstage we were in a frenzy: sets had to be changed, costumes repaired, makeup fixed; the performers had to dress, eat, and try to relax if they could.

There was always work to be done—writing comedy bits, coming up with ideas and choreography. And a couple of nights a week, we had to rehearse for the next week's show. It was a bone-crushing schedule.

But all the work was worth it, because this was a noble venture, a brand-new black entertainment showcase. It was like a new television network starting now. There is risk; there's always a chance it'll sink. But if it sails—man, nobody wants to miss that ride.

For the first show, Sussman had signed Benny Carter's orchestra and Aida Ward, famous downtown on Broadway, where she sang "I Can't Give You Anything but Love" in *Blackbirds of 1928*. He'd also gotten the comics Dusty Fletcher and Troy Brown, a dance group called the Three Rhythm Kings, a vocal trio called the Three Palmer Brothers, and the dance duet Norton and Margot.

It was up to Clarence and me to present all the talent in a unified revue, or "tab"-style format. Since our featured players were a big band and a singer, we decided to present a musical menu. So the Apollo opened with a show we called "Jazz A La Carte."

The tab format was developed by black show people as a stock company in the South in the early 1900s. Its object was a popular means of continued work—in the same venue. At the Apollo, each show opened with a newsreel and feature film. But the real entertainment began when the emcee walked out onstage to introduce the show. The band would then swing into a number. Then the Apollo Rockettes—our chorus line of "sixteen gorgeous high steppers"—would do their thing. Next would be a novelty act, a juggler, a tap dancer, or an animal act, followed by some up-and-coming young singer. After another number by the chorus, a series of comedy acts would warm up the crowd for the featured attraction to perform their big hit song. After that number came the grand finale, with everyone in the cast taking part, dancing and singing.

The ads promoting "Jazz A La Carte" mentioned that "Ralph Cooper's inimitable band" would make an appearance. But my Kongo Knights were kaput at the moment, so I earned my keep as master of ceremonies, which meant I was the headwaiter who served hot helpings of "Jazz A La Carte."

The show, thank God, was a smash. The *Age*'s Vere E. Johns was always a bit square around the edges, so I worried what he would say about the Apollo's first show. And indeed, he said he was most pleased "by the entire absence of sensuous dancing, salacious jokes and hokum." But he loved the show and predicted that "Harlem is in for a new deal in entertainment." He even had the good taste to report that "Ralph Cooper made a good entrance as emcee and kept the program moving swiftly." Johns wasn't alone. All the critics raved about the hot action down on 125th Street. The success of that opening was like a payoff for all our hard work and dedication.

But the euphoria generated by the success of "Jazz A La Carte" was short-lived. Audiences simply were not in the habit of looking for entertainment on 125th Street, which was still a business district catering to whites, where "segregation without the signs" was still being practiced. There was no active club scene; there were no black hot spots at all. It was obvious that it was going to take more than one well-received revue to get black audiences to even think about 125th Street as a place to go to and relax and be entertained.

So even after that great opening, we were playing to half-houses, even quarter-houses. If you put all four shows together, the audience might equal one full house. Some nights you could fire a cannon in the theatre and not hit a soul.

The theatre was suffering. If we could have held that audience night after night, we'd be set. But as it was, we were ready to apply for public assistance. We'd done everything but say the last rites.

The frustrating thing was that we were presenting wonderful shows. Our ads touted "the smartest colored shows" in Harlem, and they were. One week we had Bessie Smith as headliner and a fan dancer named Norma, "the sepia Mae West," on the bill along with "Harlem's own son, Ralph Cooper" and the usual lineup of comedians and dancers. Morris Sussman was booking some fine, up-and-coming acts—but nobody was coming to see them. Sussman desperately wanted the Apollo to begin to establish itself. The shows were good, the cast and crew the best. But we just weren't catching fire. It was cold and damp as a March night during those first months.

Sussman asked us all to put our heads together and come up with something that would put the Apollo on the map. There were constant brainstorming sessions, but nothing was clicking. Then, during one of our nightly skull sessions, I remembered something we did a few

A team of young hoofers do some slick stair-stepping during a production number from another one of my films, *Gangsters on the Loose*. It was choreographed by Willie Covan, who taught the Hollywood stars.

years before at the Lafayette Theatre. To keep people in the theatre on traditionally slow Wednesday nights, I started something we called Wednesday Night Auditions. These were basically amateur shows, with me acting as emcee and Norman Miller, the roly-poly stagehand everyone called Porto Rico, as the clown who shooed the booed off-stage. The auditions had become popular attractions at the Lafayette. In 1932 the *Pittsburgh Courier*'s Harlem show-business correspondent, Floyd Snelson, attended one of the shows. "It's a fact," he wrote, "that if an amateur can score on the Lafayette stage, he's marked for a glittering career."

So Sussman was saying, "We've got to fill the house *every* night, not just a couple of nights a month. How the hell are we going to do it?''

"Tell me, Morris," I said, "what's the answer worth to you?"

"I'm serious, Coop. The situation is desperate."

"Your worries are over. I got the answer—let's stage a weekly amateur show."

"Nobody's going to pay good money to see a nobody," somebody else said. "Why should I go all the way down to 125th Street to hear some stranger sing off-key when I can stay home and listen to my wife sing in the shower?"

So I told them about the opportunity shows staged over at the Lafayette. "Those shows were a hit because the audience applauded the good ones and booed the bad ones. And the amateurs were willing to take the risk of being booed because it was the only opportunity they ever got to prove their own talents."

My pitch turned into a speech. "The two most important words in the English language are 'freedom' and 'opportunity,'" I said. "Talent is freedom, and opportunity is the ability to display your talent and so exercise your freedom." It seemed to me, I said, that a regular Wednesday-night amateur night might be just the thing to save the Apollo. "Here we are in the depths of the worst economic depression in American history. Millions of people are out of work and on the dole. We can make people a unique offer: With nothing but talent and a lot of heart, you can make it. You can be somebody. That is the American dream, and it is the Harlem dream—and we can make it the Apollo dream!"

My little speech worked wonders. Morris said, "Work it out. We'll start Wednesday." But I don't think he or anybody else in the room thought it would really do the trick for the Apollo.

But I knew something they didn't. I knew that there was a warehouse of talent in Harlem just crying for opportunity. Even now, after fifty years, we haven't scratched the surface. In Harlem, everybody knows how to sing—or nearly everybody. The reason is church. Uptown, everybody goes to church, and in church, everybody sings. Most of 'em are pretty good. And a few—well, some of them you know by name. Most of the great singers of the last hundred years came out of the church. From Bessie Smith and Ella Fitzgerald, Ethel Waters and Sarah Vaughan, to Aretha Franklin and Sam Cooke and James Brown, Whitney Houston, Patti LaBelle—you name some black singer, and I'll bet you they started in church singing gospel before they became famous by switching over and singing blues or swing or soul or rock or whatever the secular music of the time happened to be. Harlem is just chock-full of church-singing school kids who dream of singing and dancing onstage. They are out there today, and they were out there fifty years ago, and they'll always be out there.

That's why I always thought Amateur Night was going to be a great success. I don't want to give the impression that I *invented* amateur contests. It's an idea that's as old as the first attempt to find out who's best. Amateur contests date back to the beginning of society, when they had competitions to find out who could light the best fire or who was the best shot or the best storyteller. Who's the best talent? Whoever's got the nerve and the verve to get up and do it.

My idea was unique in that it wasn't set up for buffoonery, to make fun of people. It's not a sideshow like the old "Gong Show" on television. Mine is not like that. Ralph Cooper's Harlem Amateur Night is a lot of fun, but its purpose is to provide opportunity. Back at the Lafayette I learned that the first critical element in staging a successful show was figuring out how to handle the losers. Poor performances are going to be booed, but nobody wants to scar some eager young kid for life. At the same time, it would be offensive to the audience to allow a dreadful singer to rape a favorite song. There had to be some humane, but funny, way to cut a hapless performer off in mid-routine and hurry him from the stage so that he could begin to work at finding a cure for whatever ailed his act.

Back at the Lafayette, I had discovered a stagehand with a peculiar talent. Norman Miller was a short, pudgy man with a big belly and an even bigger smile. He was very personable, and he had a big, uproarious laugh. Everybody called him Porto Rico because he was so portly. When I staged the first audition night at the Lafayette, just for fun I wrote Porto Rico into the show. He was supposed to come out in different outlandish costumes and hustle losing contestants off the stage. And he was wonderful.

I had urged Sussman to hire Miller at the Apollo because he was fun to have around and an excellent stagehand—his presence would build camaraderie and good spirit. So the whole time we were wracking our brains trying to find the key to the Apollo's success, he was right there, bumping into walls backstage and making everybody laugh. Inspiration struck, and I had a little talk with Porto Rico. He agreed to reprise his old role and become Harlem Amateur Night's official Executioner.

Porto Rico put a head full of creativity into his crazy costumes. He'd dress up like a hermit and chase people with a pitchfork; he'd dress like a jungle native and go after them with a spear; he'd be a farmer with a shotgun or an old lady with a broom. He'd always do a funny little dervish, and he brought the house down every time. But he never "hooked" the contestants or pushed them. I don't believe he ever even touched them. And this was a very important thing—because one thing I didn't want was for it to be a humiliation contest. Years later, when they were about to reopen the Apollo in 1983, someone asked me what kind of hook I was going to use to yank losers from the stage. "We're not going to use any kind of hook," I said. "When we started Amateur Night years ago, we didn't use a hook. I doubt we need one now."

In order to make the format work, you have to consider the amateur, whether he's a future star or a forever schlemiel. And the fact is, it's a lot more likely that he is *not* a future star.

There's always a truckload of reasons why amateurs fail. They can go off-key. They can lose the beat. They can forget the words. They can sweat so bad that they freeze. Whatever happens, they're probably just plain scared to death. Now the audience is dictator, and if they're booing, I can't stop them, even if the person getting booed isn't as bad as the audience likes to think. So if the audience wants them run off, we're gonna run them off—but not with a hook. A hook is demeaning, humiliating. It's kicking them when they're down. We want to give the contest a sense of fun. And with Porto Rico running the bad talent off, everybody laughs—even the contestants, because they know folks aren't laughing at them, but at Porto Rico in his outrageous old-lady outfit.

When somebody gets run off, it's fun time. There's a lot of energy in the theatre, because the audience is up jumping and screaming. The clown is going crazy, and we're cranking up the siren, and the band is playing up-tempo and swinging, and I'm all over the stage hollering. So as the amateur is being escorted off, everybody's having a good time. And the amateur doesn't leave the stage ashamed of himself. He doesn't feel like he's been kicked.

★   ★   ★

Alice Whitman of the famous Whitman Sisters Show. A top revue attraction on the TOBA, Alice was an outstanding tap dancer.

The most important ingredient for the show is the presence of a charismatic emcee. Without a warm rapport between the audience and the emcee, the whole show can sink. And when that happens, the stage and everybody on it feels like the *Titanic* after they ran into the ice.

My good friend the actor and comedian Baron Wilson remembers what the Apollo was like when we opened in 1934. "Even then, in the very beginning, the Apollo had the toughest audience there was in any theatre I've ever worked, especially that top balcony. A seat just cost a quarter up there, but it might as well have been a hundred dollars. The kids up there were demanding. They wanted their money's worth. They were so tough some acts would go out front or to the backstage door where the kids would gather before a show and pay the kids off so they wouldn't get booed offstage. And I'm talking about the professionals, not the amateurs.

"Ralph was always known for his special charisma. He could walk out in front of that audience and they were his. Even that top balcony would be quiet. He could talk to them down-to-earth. That was his baby—handling that crazy audience."

Man, it's just amazing that the older Baron gets, the smarter he gets.

Seriously, I appreciate what he says, and I include it here not to blow my own trumpet (not entirely, anyway) but to explain why I was born to create and to host Amateur Night in Harlem. An emcee has to be someone the contestants trust and the audience knows and respects. An arrogant and pompous emcee who belittles contestants or the audience is making arrangements for his cremation onstage. One more toast before you roast. I've had guest emcees come out who are experienced show and radio people who knock 'em dead in other theatres, but for one reason or another they're the ones who do the dying on our stage. If they don't get run off, they can slow the whole thing to a walk. Without the emcee's energy to sustain the pace, the whole show will fall apart.

You got to have rapport, and that's one thing I knew I had. After more than fifteen years in show business, I had developed a stage style that worked. I was basically a low-key-type entertainer who dressed in style, tasteful, sharp. I even heard the women say I was handsome, "the height of sartorial and tonsorial splendor." But I was humorous, down-to-earth, not a pompous type and not a buffoon. Today you'd call it hip—and that's what we called it back then, too.

There's something else I know about performance that I didn't learn onstage. I learned it in the water. When I was fifteen, I was a third-class lifeguard, a glorified name for janitor, down on the New Jersey shore at Asbury Park beach. Third-class guards did all the work, cleaning and raking the sand and storing the equipment. And on top of all that, we had to save the drowning.

When you go to save someone, the first thing you have to remember is that most people don't drown from inability. They drown from fright. That's the first thing you learn. So you don't approach them from the front. If you come up facing them, they'll try to drown you. They'll try to climb up over the top of your head to get out of the water. So you always have to approach them from the back. Or if you happen to find yourself in front and they start scrambling, you have to take them down under water so you can control them. Then you get around back, get a firm hold on them, and start talking to them.

Even the most talented swimmer can panic and drown. And it's possible to drown on dry land, as a lot of people have found out on our stage. I think that knowledge helped me better understand what the most talented amateurs go through trying to keep their stage fright in check out on that stage in front of that demanding audience. You can get a jolt of pure panic walking out into that spotlight. The first few times you do it, it's like grabbing a live wire in your bare hands. It's like holding a limp fire hose and suddenly somebody turns the hydrant on full blast. If you're not prepared for it, the force can knock you off your feet and send you flying. So you have to hype yourself up before you get onstage. You have to brace yourself for the full-force shock you're about to receive.

As we fine-tuned the Amateur Night plans, we decided on a theme song: "I May Be Wrong, But I Think You're Wonderful." I thought that had the right touch of humor. It was what the contestants wanted to believe—"I may be wrong, but the audience thinks I'm wonderful." We also decided right off that the audience would be the dictator of who wins and who loses. All the acts that were not booed and run off would come back onstage at the end of the show. Each act would take a bow, and whoever got the biggest response was winner.

As for musical accompaniment, we decided to use whatever big-name orchestra was booked in the theatre that week. That way, the amateurs not only got to perform before a sophisticated audience, they had the added treat of singing onstage with the Count Basie Orchestra, or Jimmie Lunceford's band, or Duke Ellington's, or Louis Armstrong's.

And we decided that winners would be awarded something better than prize money—further opportunity. Amateur Night winners would be given a week's engagement at the Apollo Theatre. If someone came onstage Wednesday and won, they would appear in next week's show.

Around the time the Apollo first opened, the city of New York widened Seventh Avenue—a good idea, which relieved the congestion created by a rapidly swelling number of automobiles. But that bit of practical progress also caused the soul of Harlem to shrink a little, because the widening meant that the shade trees that had lined the Boulevard of Dreams and lent their beauty to Harlem since the community was born a lifetime before would have to be removed. One of the trees sacrificed in the name of progress was a landmark of Harlem and a symbol of the promise the community held for millions of African-Americans. For as long as anyone could remember, the Tree of Hope had stood on the broad sidewalk on the east side of Seventh Avenue between 131st and 132nd streets. The tree shaded the backstage alley entrance to the Lafayette Theatre and Connie's Inn, two of the most popular live entertainment showcases in Harlem. It was the social center of Harlem's show-business community, a place where older performers, all braggadocio and swagger, would gain inspiration from one another while their younger would-be competitors stood wide-eyed, their jaws hanging open as they listened to the old pros boasting about how much money they were making and how bright their stars burned in the firmament. Any time some unknown was plucked from the group and given a last-minute opening on a local chorus line or in a road show about to leave town on the Theatre Owners' Booking Association (TOBA) chitlin circuit which operated ostensibly in the South, he would be congratulated by the old pros, slapped on the back and welcomed to their number. Then he would seal his connection to the group by wrapping his arms around the thick trunk of the Tree of Hope and give thanks for a Harlem promise fulfilled.

So it was a sad moment in Harlem when the Tree of Hope was uprooted and chopped up for firewood. None of us performers could bear to see it off without a proper burial. So we enlisted Bill ''Bojangles'' Robinson, the so-called mayor of Harlem, and his fellow mayor Fiorello La Guardia to lead a ceremony in which we placed a bronze plaque in the pavement that covered the ground where the tree once stood. Bill hoped the plaque would take the place of the tree and the spot would remain a gathering place for show people.

But it never happened—maybe simply because the sidewalk wasn't as wide as it used to be, or because there were no branches to shade us dandies from the sun. Whatever the reason, it didn't happen. And somebody had an idea to transplant the roots of the tree to the traffic island in the middle of Seventh Avenue, but no new shoot ever broke through the ground.

Once the tree was sawed up for firewood, somebody got the idea of selling the pieces as souvenirs. So I got myself a piece. It was only about eighteen inches across and a foot high—an ordinary hunk of wood. But it meant something to me, and I took it back to the Apollo. I had the thing sitting in my dressing room, and just before the first Amateur Night, I asked Phil Pearman, the backstage carpenter, to sand and shellac the log and mount it on an Ionic column. We placed the pedestal stage right, just outside the curtain, so the audience could see it. It became a tradition of Amateur Night to have each contestant touch the tree on the way to center stage.

I don't know how many people actually believed the wood had any real power as a talisman, but they rubbed it just the same. Some ran both hands back and forth over the log as fast as they could, like they thought a genie would pop out. Others paused and rested one hand on the tree limb and took a deep, calming breath. Some just absently slapped at it in passing, and some kissed their fingertips before touching them to the log. Some actually leaned over and kissed the wood with their lips on their way to the microphone. Just about every single performer who appeared in Amateur Night touched that log one way or another. Within a year or two, the log was smooth as a sea stone from all the hands rubbing it. It was a nice sort of ceremonial thing, which allowed everyone to think about their common heritage; it made every amateur feel a part of a rich show-business history.

But in later years, I began to feel that the Tree of Hope was antiquated. I felt it was superstitious—too much the kind of thing attributed to blacks in those days. There was an old routine from white vaudeville where a guy puts on a white sheet and goes ''Boo!'' and twenty blacks jump out of the window and run around in circles and carry on because they saw the sheet and thought it was a ghost. The tradition of touching the Tree of Hope for good luck seemed to me to hark back to that kind of demeaning, stereotypical thinking; and so after a few years, I had it removed from the stage.

But in the beginning there was a hunk of the Tree of Hope sitting on a pedestal in front of the stage-right curtain, and every amateur who walked out on the Apollo stage to face that sometimes ferocious audience touched the tree for good luck. Maybe it really did give the kids the added strength they needed to take the shock waiting for them in the spotlight. As long as they believed, it worked.

As soon as Sussman gave me the go-ahead, I started making the announcement at every show, inviting audience members to come around to Monday auditions if they wanted to test their own talents and to tell their friends about Amateur Night in Harlem. Every week Sussman took out ads in the local papers announcing "the smartest colored shows" in Harlem at the Apollo. That first week he added a brief note in small type at the bottom of the ads: "Wednesday Night: Ralph Cooper's Amateur Night in Harlem."

The week we started we had a truly surreal lineup. Louis Armstrong's wife Lil Hardin (billed as "Mrs. Louis Armstrong"), a great pianist, and her band, were headlining. But the people everyone was talking about that week was a roster of acts from a traveling freak show that had appeared at the Chicago World's Fair in 1932. Imagine what those poor amateur contestants must have been thinking down in the Green Room as the audience upstairs went wild over the Needle Mystery Man, who swallowed needle and thread and regurgitated a threaded needle?

Downstairs, the Tattoo Girl, with three hundred and fifty tattoos on her near-naked body, was walking around the Green Room while the housewives and school kids and truck drivers who showed up for our first amateur contest looked on in disbelief. They also got to meet Sealo, the Seal Boy, a small crippled kid with withered arms, and an armless girl who got a standing ovation for the dexterity she demonstrated with her toes. There was a contortionist billed as the India Rubber Man, and an Elephant Skin Girl. But the most bizarre act was an enormous, 420-pound fat lady called the Personality Girl. Her entire act consisted of doing the shimmy by walking fast across stage, stopping suddenly, and letting her dancing flab do the rest.

But none of the freakishness seemed to hurt the amateur hour. At eleven p.m., after the last show of the regular program, the band struck up the Amateur Night theme, "I May Be Wrong," and I came out, "Good evening, ladies and gentlemen, and welcome to the one and only Amateur Night in Harlem. I may be wrong, but I think you're going to love the show we have for you tonight."

I told them the rules: "If you like the performer, cheer. You know how to cheer, don't you?" And the audience let out a roar that rattled windows all over Harlem. "But if you feel they need a little woodshedding, don't be shy. Let 'em know loud and clear. You know how to boo, don't you?" Did they ever! They booed like they'd been waiting all their lives to blow folk offstage.

Before introducing the first contestant, I told the audience about the Tree of Hope, how it was a symbol of dreams come true and how it was sadly removed from its place on the Boulevard of Dreams. But we were lucky, I said, to have a piece of the tree here with us tonight. And as the spotlight hit the tree, I said, "And now, with no further ado, let me introduce you to our very first amateur contestant. We want you to come on out here, son—but on your way, be sure and stop by that pedestal and touch all that is left of the world-famous Tree of Hope."

No one jumped from obscurity to stardom that night. There was a schoolteacher who sang a gospel song, a delivery boy who tap-danced, and a fat man who shimmied like the Personality Girl and got chased by Porto Rico for his efforts. But from that night on, Amateur Night in Harlem was a tremendous success. As the hipsters of the day would say, it was twenty-one—the very best. It was the real deal McNeal, the tops, pops.

Word got out faster than the horses at Belmont. We had twice as many amateur talents the second week as we had the first. And everybody in the audience must have told ten people, because the next week's amateur show was a sellout. Before long, people started bringing noisemakers into the theatre with them and even trumpets and bugles. One night a guy tried to haul an upright piano in with him.

Once word was out around town, Harlem's critics began dropping by the theatre to see the amateur show. Even old Vere E. Johns admitted that "as much as I hate jazz," he was surprised, amazed, dazzled, and enthralled by our amateur show. He wrote:

> The audience acted as judge and it was up to them to approve or disapprove according to how the particular act appealed to them. Strange as it may seem, the audience made very accurate decisions. One or two

of the performers really had no business on the stage at all, but one can admire them for their courage if for nothing else.

The audience did not hesitate for a moment. They spotted a lousy act the moment it started and booed and hissed and catcalled until the Old Man of the Mountains [Porto Rico was in his hermit's outfit that night] appeared and carried the victim off to be shot in the wings [!]. They were a little tolerant of women and children, but a man had to have something to get by.

A white candidate was treated so badly that I sympathized with him. [Can you imagine that?!] He came out to render "Pardon My Southern Accent," but the audience did not pardon his appearance and he never even got in a word. It was not because he was white that caused it, but because he was really lousier than lousy.

Johns concluded his account by mentioning that "a little song and dance kid" won, while "an ambitious little boy whose act was wire walking" made a good showing. Then, as if in defense of the Executioner summoning boo birds, Johns said that "in other countries, 75 percent of our so called performers would be greeted not only with boos, hisses and catcalls, but ripe tomatoes, cabbage heads and rotten eggs as well, before they had been on stage 30 seconds." Vere was square, but I loved that review.

I figured that if he approved of the audience's behavior, we were home free. Amateur Night never would have succeeded if the audience had been a sit-on-your-hands-and-clap-politely-type crowd. Lucky for us, the Apollo audience was far too rude for polite company. But right from the beginning, they proved themselves knowledgeable as well. They understood entertainment. They understood rhythm. They knew when you were jivin', and they were very responsive to good and bad. They would let you know how they felt. There was no sitting on the fence.

Johns's review was solid evidence that the amateur show not only was working but was a resounding success. Reading it made me feel so good, in fact, that it generated another idea. In those days, people got their evening entertainment, as well as music and news, from radio. It was common practice among the radio networks to air live music broadcasts from the great ballrooms and concert halls of New York and Chicago and other cities. The Cotton Club's worldwide fame was due at least in part to the live radio broadcasts that originated there starring Duke Ellington and later Cab Calloway. When the Apollo opened, Jimmie Lunceford was broadcasting live from the Cotton Club. But the idea of putting amateur talent on live radio had never occurred to anyone before—mainly because it seemed like a crazy stunt. If I had suggested it to people around the Apollo, they would not have said they think I'm nuts; they would have fitted me for the straightjacket.

So when I went down to see Charlie Stark, the general manager of WMCA radio in Manhattan, I didn't tell anyone I was doing it. Charlie said he never had heard of Amateur Night in Harlem. I told him Amateur Night was the greatest entertainment in the world. I said that one day it would be the equivalent of "The Amos and Andy Show," which was the top radio show at the time. Charlie laughed. He wanted to know if I needed a glass of water—was I feeling faint? It took a whole lot of talking, but after a long conversation, Charlie agreed to come uptown the following Wednesday and see the show for himself.

This was October 1934, nine months since the Apollo opened for business. We had only done two or three amateur shows, but already we knew it was working. I knew if I could just get this thing out on the air, it would hit. Once people heard that audience carrying on, they'd be hooked—I was sure of it.

Before we started Amateur Night, people used to come in to the theatre for the noon show and they'd bring a lunch and they wouldn't leave until midnight. They'd have spent their whole lives in the theatre if they could. And the first couple of Wednesdays, they stayed all day to see the amateur show at eleven. So we decided to cut the dinner performance, close the theatre at six o'clock, and put everybody out. Then we cleaned up and filled the theatre to capacity for the eight o'clock show, which would segue into the amateur show, which would begin and go out live on the air at eleven.

The show Charlie Stark saw was just an average show—which is to say it was a wild, exciting show. The audience didn't like one of the first acts on, and they started screaming and hollering so loud you could hear them all the way down on Forty-second Street. The next act came on and got a standing ovation.

After the show, Charlie came backstage and I said, "How'd you like the spectacle?"

"Well," he said, "you're going to have to fix a few things and get the timing down right."

My heart sank. I thought the show was a real winner. I had been counting on Stark's giving us the go-ahead. So I was disappointed. But I promised him that we'd work on the timing.

"Yeah," he said, "you're going to have to have a strong show next week, because you're going to be on the air."

Well, I just about jumped out of my Florsheims. And when I told Morris Sussman about it, he couldn't believe his ears.

The funny thing is, neither Morris nor I once mentioned money—not to Charlie Stark and not between ourselves. The subject never came up. But the truth is that Charlie Stark had just made a very sweet deal for himself. He was getting himself a hit show for free. At absolutely no cost to himself beyond the expense of rigging a live feed, he was getting a full production, with name stars. There was no provision that Charlie or WMCA would pay us a penny—and they didn't. But Morris and I thought of the broadcast as publicity for the Apollo Theatre that we couldn't have bought anywhere. I figured as long as the show originated at the Apollo, that would do the trick for our business. And I was right. Later, when I found out Charlie was syndicating the shows on a network of twenty-one affiliated radio stations around the country, I still felt it was good for the Apollo. Now I think I was crazy not to get the station to pay us something for what turned out to be the highest-rated nighttime show in all New York.

The next week we went on the air at eleven. It was all surprisingly simple. WMCA's technicians knew all about remote broadcasting, and everything went smoothly, without a hitch.

I only changed a few elements in the program for the live broadcast. I had to give my introduction twice. For the radio audience, I said, "Ladies and gentlemen, welcome to Amateur Night in Harlem. This is Ralph Cooper broadcasting live from the stage of the Apollo Theatre in New York City!"

I made one mistake during that first broadcast. I had a hot hoofer on ten minutes into the live show. He was fantastic. He did speed tapping, some jumps and splits, and the audience loved it. Then, for his exit, he did a backwards slide, which ever since Michael Jackson did it on TV has become known as the moonwalk. It was an easy backwards slide that a lot of comics used to do in the old days. The audience loved that dancer, but it wasn't until he was moonwalking offstage that I realized the radio audience didn't have a clue to what was going on in the show. All they could hear was the orchestra and the audience reaction. So from then on I had to remember to put dancers on before we went out over the air.

I had to describe Porto Rico's costumes on air, but that was relatively easy, since he made himself up such outlandish guises. Listeners could hear the sirens going and the stage guns firing and the audience screaming and stomping their feet so hard people's radios must have started jumping all over New York. It wasn't hard for listeners to imagine that people were having a helluva time up there in Harlem at the Apollo Theatre.

And it wasn't just radio fans and members of the audience who got into the swing of our show. Even staid old jazz hater V. E. Johns jumped on the bandwagon and praised the Apollo's Amateur Hour for opening up a new career path for the youth of Harlem to follow.

4

The Glorification of the Apollo

★ ★

When Amateur Night in Harlem went out over the air at eleven p.m. each Wednesday, every gin mill in New York, every taxicab, newsstand, and corner coffee shop, as well as the folks out on their stoops, had the radio blasting and tuned to our show on WMCA. You could walk down any street in town and that's all you heard—and not just in Harlem, but all over New York and most of the country.

Because the show was broadcast over a network of twenty-one affiliate stations, the Apollo and its Amateur Night became known throughout the United States. The Amateur Night radio show glorified the Apollo and made it famous as a proving ground for fresh young talent and, in turn, as a showcase for established stars. Count Basie, Duke Ellington, Chick Webb, Louis Prima, Louis Armstrong, Earl Hines, or whoever was playing the Apollo that week appeared on the show, performing his current hit and backing the amateurs. It was truly a fantastic thing—here were the biggest, most successful, and sophisticated orchestras in the country, swinging behind some unknown singers shaking in their shoes.

The radio broadcasts made Amateur Night the talk of the town. It was like the first season of "Saturday Night Live" when that show was the most talked-about entertainment in show business. As quick as you could say *"Live* from the Apollo Theatre!" we became the happenin' place to be. By the third or fourth broadcast, all the in crowd were streaming uptown to see what all the excitement was about. We had people coming uptown who six months before didn't even know the Apollo existed.

The downtowners would come for the amateur show, but they'd catch the regular revue too. And most had never before seen anything quite like our shows.

The carriage trade's fox-trotters could count on getting their minds blown at least once before the Amateur Hour began. Novelty acts like Doctor Sausage and the Five Pork Chops or the Three Businessmen of Rhythm joined Apollo favorites like shapely Florence Hill, who was famous for her stage costumes, which were said to be constructed from just "three square inches of red silk." Collegians venturing uptown to see a superstar like Duke Ellington and his world-famous band backing Ivie Anderson, "Harlem's blazing torch song sensation," would be introduced to an act like Stuff Smith on the same bill. Stuff played a very sophisticated jazz violin, but his big hit was a song called "I'se A Muggin' " in which he'd lead the audience in a rocking and grunting caveman routine: "One, two, three, *uh-uh-uh*, four, five, six, *oo-oo-ooh.*" Then there was the inimitable Pig-meat Markham, a great Apollo comic who started the Truckin' dance craze with his shuffling exit step. Every week we put on shows that folks wouldn't soon forget.

There was never any animosity between the downtowners and the uptowners in the audience. For the whites, it was exciting and new. And the blacks welcomed them because their presence meant that black talents were being recognized and appreciated outside the black community.

One of the things that made Amateur Night such a success was the fast-paced sense of surprise—the feeling that anything could happen. There was no way of knowing if the Executioner was going to make an appearance, and that created suspense for both the audience at the theatre and all those people listening in on radio. The only promise I could make was a one-hundred-percent guarantee that nothing was one hundred percent guaranteed. I never knew with any certainty if an audience was going to love an act or boo it to Hoboken. After looking over the list of talent before a show, I might say to Porto Rico, "You're gonna have an easy night tonight, Porto Rico. You're just gonna be a spectator. The audience is going to love all these contestants''—and most of them would get run off. There was just no way of predicting. So I long ago stopped saying who I thought would win and who wouldn't.

But that didn't go down well with the radio producers, who hated the unknown. They naturally wanted to be prepared, so they were always asking me who was hot and who was not. I'd have to tell them I just didn't know, which is not what they wanted to hear. All I could do was arrange the lineup so the ones I thought might do well weren't lumped together at the beginning or end of the show. If I heard some good voices during auditions, I'd place them in the show at intervals. But I can't control the emotions of the audience. Once they get up a head of steam, there's nothing to do but jump for cover. If they have their blood up, Mother Teresa could walk out there, make her plea for starving babies, and still get booed off the stage.

One youngster I was convinced would win in a walk was almost run off her first minute out there. She came this close to nowhere. But as it turned out, she was one of the biggest stars ever to get a start on the amateur show. Today it's hard to imagine Ella Fitzgerald ever stumbling on any song—she's such a smart, capable performer. But when she made her first appearance here in 1934, she was just a fifteen-year-old girl. Ella was born in Newport News, Virginia, but she grew up in Yonkers, where her mama moved after Ella's daddy died when she was just a little baby. Ella spent some time in the Riverdale Orphanage. Ella's mama died shortly after her first Apollo appearance and Chick Webb adopted her.

Ella has said that she had planned to do a dance number that night, but when she saw a really hot dance group compete ahead of her, she changed her mind. At the last minute she decided to sing a Connee Boswell song, ''The Object of My Affection.''

I should have known that even Ella, whose confidence was anchored in real talent, could be blown off course by a sudden and furious gust of fear. And that's just what happened. ''I'm always nervous when I start to sing,'' Ella told a newspaper reporter a few years later. ''Sometimes I can't even remember the words and then I get along on riffs. Mostly I picture what I'm singing. If it's a river, then I get a picture in my mind of a river.''

But Ella's visions failed her that night at the Apollo. She came out onstage all jumpy and unnerved. She told that reporter that she

My Harlem Amateur Night at the Apollo became world famous for launching talented young performers to stardom. One of the first and most talented of all, Ella Fitzgerald, was just fifteen when she came to dance but sang instead.

first tried to do a little dance step, but she was so intimidated by the audience, her feet felt like they were stuck in cement. When she started to sing, she was off-key, and her voice sounded like a hoarse croak.

I could feel the audience start to rumble. They didn't boo immediately, but I could feel the blood rising. So I stopped Ella in the opening verse and said, "Folks, hold on now. This young lady's got a gift she'd like to share with us tonight. She's just having a little trouble getting it out of its wrapper. Let's give her a second chance.''

That's all the help Ella Fitzgerald needed. As soon as she composed herself, she tore the place apart. She found her voice and the audience loved her and made her that night's twenty-five-dollar winner with a week's appearance at the theatre. But, of importance, Chick Webb hired Ella as his vocalist on the spot. At Chick's next recording session, Ella recorded, ''A-Tisket A-Tasket'' and gold and fame poured into her basket.

Seven years later, in 1941, Ella returned to the Apollo to perform in Amateur Night. But this time she was the leader of the headlining act—the Ella Fitzgerald Orchestra. And a new crop of young hopeful amateurs were very nervous to be singing on the same stage as the First Lady of Jazz.

Chick Webb was another member of jazz's royal family. He was an ace stick man. He also happened to be extremely short, with a slight hunch to his back. He was long on humor, though, and we used to do a running gag every time he worked the Apollo. He'd be ensconced behind his drum set and I'd say to him, ''Take a bow, Chick.'' And he'd stand up at his drums and take a bow. I'd say, ''C'mon, man, take a bow.'' He'd bow again. I'd say, ''What's a matter with you? Get up and take a bow, man!'' And Chick would finally shout, ''I *am* standing up—what are you talking about?'' The audience would fall out. But because that gag wouldn't work on radio, we ran it before the broadcast.

Just five years after he backed Ella on our amateur show, Chick Webb died. He was only thirty-two years old. He died in Baltimore after a kidney operation. I don't know if the operation was botched or what. But I'll always remember reading about it in the downtown newspapers. I wish Chick could have lived to see integration. Maybe then he would have been paid the respect he deserved. The New York *Sun* reported that ''all of Darktown went into mourning'' after learning of the death of ''the little colored boy with hunched shoulders.'' The *Post* tried to appear ''with it'': FAMED MAESTRO FOR RUG CUTTERS DIES. The black papers reported the tragedy in more somber tones— and with greater accuracy. Chick was just seventeen when Duke Ellington hired him to play in his band, a reporter remembered. Chick went on to become renowned as ''the world's fastest swing drummer.'' Author of such classic jazz numbers as ''Stompin' at the Savoy" and "Have Mercy," Chick was best remembered, one paper said, for his discovery of Ella Fitzgerald "in a Harlem amateur contest." Ella sang at Chick's funeral. (I should add Chick was the greatest cymbal man in the country, a truly respected musician.)

Ever since Prohibition ended and the club scene waned, uptown habitués Mae West, Damon Runyon, and Burgess Meredith had fallen out of the Harlem habit. It took Harlem Amateur Night to bring them back. Walter Winchell became a big fan of our show, and once he started plugging our show in his own very popular show-biz news-and-gossip radio program, the Apollo became the place to be seen on Wednesday nights. At the beginning of each show, before we went out on the air, I would look out at the audience and see stars like Georgie Jessel and Martha Raye, Joan Crawford and Dorothy Kilgallen, the top movie, radio, and stage stars of the day. Their agents and managers would call a week in advance to reserve orchestra seats for the stars and their entourages. Betty Grable would stop traffic when she'd walk into the theatre lobby in one of her long slit skirts.

I began the tradition of introducing the visiting stars out of necessity. One night Jimmy Durante was sitting in the stage-right box. I was used to seeing celebrities in the audience, and I didn't say anything about it—I assumed they wanted their privacy. But during the radio broadcast, somebody in the audience started shouting "Schnozzola—Schnozzola—Schnozzola." A whole bunch of people thought this was funny and joined in chanting Durante's nickname. I had to introduce Durante and get him to take a bow in order to quiet the audience so we could go on with the show. But Durante didn't mind a bit. He stood up and we put the spotlight on him and he turned to give the crowd a look at his famous profile.

From then on, I would always introduce guests, and it became a regular feature of the radio show. People began to look forward to hearing which of the top stars of the day made it to the show that week. Eddie Cantor, Bob Hope, Jackie Gleason, Milton Berle, Jack Benny all took bows during the broadcast. Many times, getting them to stand at their seat and take a bow wasn't enough, partly because of the way the Apollo is built: the rake is so sharp that if you're seated in the orchestra, even two or three rows back, the upper balcony can't see you. So if the celebrity was popular enough—or the response was loud enough—I invited the star to come up onstage and take a bow.

One night I noticed Ray Noble, the renowned London orchestra leader who composed the classic hits "Goodnight, Sweetheart" and "The Very Thought of You," watching the show from a box. Box seats were held for stars and personalities. During the broadcast, I introduced "the famous orchestra leader from London, now playing the Rainbow Room in Radio City—Ray Noble!" The audience went wild. I didn't think that many people even knew who Ray Noble was. But he seemed to have an extremely enthusiastic audience in Harlem. Then he walked onstage and the audience went dumb. Finally someone yelled, "We thought you said Noble Sissle, Coop!"

Jack Benny used to come up with Eddie Anderson, who played Rochester. Backstage over the PA Jack would call out in his familiar deadpan voice, "Oh, Rochester!" Eddie would answer in the raspy voice that was even more famous than Benny's, "Yessir, Mr. Benny." That was enough to win a standing ovation. People didn't need to see them to love them. Then Benny would walk out onstage and say, "Where are my green socks?" Or he'd say, "Where'd you get your name, Rochester?" "I was born in Syracuse, Mr. Benny," Eddie would reply. The crowd always just went wild.

Some stars walked out onstage to take their bows and I would have a helluva time getting them off once they heard the kind of applause that audience gave out.

Eddie Cantor was a huge star in those days. He was playing the Loews Paradise on the Grand Concourse and I went by to see him one night between shows. He was very gracious and said he had heard great things about my show on WMCA. I said, "You know, you have a lot of people that love you in our community even though you never perform in Harlem. The people uptown don't get many chances to see you, so why don't you drop by next Wednesday?"

But Eddie wasn't sure about it. "What would I do?" he said.

"You just come and sit in the box and let the people know you're there. Let them see you wave at them. Say hello. That's all."

Eddie finally agreed, and on the following Wednesday, he arrived at the theatre and we got him seated just before the radio broadcast began. At around eleven-thirty, when there was a station break, I told the folks, "There's a man with us tonight, one of the true greats of show business—ladies and gentlemen, Mr. Eddie Cantor!"

Well, he stood up in his box and we put the spotlight on him and the people started chanting, "We want Can-tor! We want Cantor!'' The whole house took up the chant, and it lasted through the commercial, and when we came back on the air, people listening in had no idea what was going on. So I introduced Eddie again, and he got out of that box and on to the stage in record time. He went to the mike and said, ''Never in my entire career have I ever received an ovation as thunderous and exciting as this that you're giving me. Now, I'm gonna take full advantage of it. I'm gonna sing.'' With that the audience went bonkers. They screamed for him. At twelve o'clock, when we went off the air, Cantor was still onstage entertaining.

Nights like that were a big boost for the theatre. The next morning I would overhear conversations around town. ''Hey, man, Jackie Gleason was at the Apollo last night.''

''Yeah, I heard him on the air.''

''Oh, they were screamin' and hollerin' in there like you wouldn't believe!''

''I've *got* to get up there to Harlem and catch that show!''

It got to a point where nobody in show business dared to miss the show at the Apollo.

The Apollo soon became famous for our comedy bits. Half the stars in vaudeville used to come up here looking for new material. Milton Berle came so often, he started bringing his secretary along to take notes on what we were doing. But all these bits he saw here had to be rewritten for his audience. He couldn't take a bit designed for a black audience and run with it on his show. He'd have to fashion it to suit his audience's tastes. A lot of our humor was double entendre, stuff that was a little too racy for middle-American radio. But Milton would steal anything—still does. I love him, though. He's a great, great performer. Eddie Cantor is another one who got bits from us. I never felt any resentment at all. It was an honor. Besides, I'd be just as quick to steal something from them!

I learned way back that the secret to a long life is to see the humor in things. It was an Apollo rocket that carried Neil Armstrong to the moon, but when he didn't call and say thanks for the lift, I didn't get mad.

Speaking of ''to the moon,'' Jackie Gleason was a big Apollo fan. Jackie took my breakaway step and used it throughout his career. It was the little step he made when he'd say, ''And away we go!'' That was his line, but it was my step. I always used it when I made my entrance. But Jackie was a nice guy, and I never resented him.

He used to call up and say, "Hey, Coop, I'm comin' up there to get something tonight, so make sure it's a good show."

One guy who never confessed his thievery was Benny Goodman's brother-in-law, John Hammond, the record producer, who used to come up all the time and "discover" talent. That was his polite word for it. When he saw performers on our stage, he quickly realized that if they went over with our audience, they'd go over anywhere. So he'd take them downtown, sign them up for Columbia Records, and tell the world he discovered them. One of the stars Hammond claimed to have discovered was Billie Holiday. He introduced her to Goodman, who cut a couple of sides with her. Neither song went anywhere, and Billie was dropped by Hammond and Goodman and forgotten.

Some histories refer to Billie Holiday as an Amateur Night winner. She really wasn't. But she did get her big break at the Apollo, and I was the gambler who put her on.

One night in 1935, I went up to a joint called Hot Cha's for some spaghetti. Hot Cha's was a little bar and grill up at 134th Street and Seventh Avenue, and I had heard they served some great food. I didn't know they even had entertainment, but I saw they had this little two-by-four stage, and this tall girl came out and sang a number. I was there for the spaghetti, so I didn't pay much attention. Besides, I spent all day around show people. I wanted to get away from singers, and now here came one to ruin my dinner.

Then she started singing "Them There Eyes." That's when I noticed that she was young and pretty, with a lovely smile, and she had a voice like I had never heard before. She sang with a kind of crying style. Before I knew it, my fork was on the table and my food was getting cold and I didn't care. She finished that song and started a second number, "When the Moon Turns Green." It was fantastic. I forgot all about that great spaghetti.

I talked to the restaurant manager and told him I wanted to put her onstage at the Apollo Theatre. A year earlier, he would have said, "The what?" But now, because of the radio show and the huge success we were having, he was ecstatic. I said I'd be sure to mention where I found this singer. He said he would pick her up and carry her down to the Apollo for me if I'd do that.

The next day was April 19, 1935. Billie was just twenty years old, and when she arrived at the theatre, she was wearing a plain, drab dress that looked rather ordinary. She was tall and pretty, but

Billie Holiday never went anywhere without her two Chihuahuas. Man, they could do some yapping, but I didn't mind as long as I could listen to their mama sing. Years after I helped Billie launch her star at the Apollo, she dropped by the old Palm Cafe, where I was hosting a radio show, to say hello. The woman in white is Ruth Bowen, who managed the great Dinah Washington and, later, Aretha Franklin.

there was no gardenia in her hair, and her clothes had none of the low-cut glamour that later became her signature.

I said, "Where's your stage costume, Billie?"

"You're looking at it," she said.

I gave her fifty dollars and sent her across the street with one of the chorus girls, and she came back in a white satin gown and evening slippers. She was pretty as a spring day, but she was so skinny and looked so inexperienced that Clarence Robinson thought I had gone crazy. He had a master eye for talent, so I worried a little when he pulled me aside and said, "Coop, listen, man, I hate to say it, but this girl is nothing. She's got nothing. You don't want to put her on. I heard her in rehearsal. She's like a crooning bird. She's afraid of a large audience. She'll embarrass you and she'll embarrass the theatre. Listen to me, man. Take my advice. Give her a few dollars and send her back where you found her."

I told Clarence he was the crazy one. "She's great, man. You been workin' too hard. You've lost your ear." But I had my doubts. I wondered, "What if he's right?" So I asked around, and everybody who heard her in rehearsal said they weren't sure about her, either. They didn't know if she could cut it. Still, I had a gut feeling. I knew I had never heard singing so low, so lazy, and so sexy. I knew that everyone out front would love her once they heard her.

At noon, after the first picture, I went out to introduce the show. Because she was untested, Billie was supposed to go on first. I told the lunch crowd the story about how I went up to Hot Cha's for spaghetti and came back with a singer who was a feast with all the fixins. "But," I said, "a lot of people don't agree with me that this girl is sensational. They think I'm out of my mind about this singer. I'm gonna let you be the judge. Ladies and gentlemen—let's hear a twenty-one-gun Apollo welcome for Miss Billie Holiday!"

In her autobiography, Billie says she was so terrified that morning in the wings that Pigmeat had to give her a shove to get her out onstage. She told me she was always scared of big crowds and big theatres. But from the moment she walked out onstage and opened her mouth, I knew she was going to be a huge, huge star. That day was blast-off time for Billie Holiday.

There are singers and there are what I call delineators or storytellers. Billie Holiday was a delineator. She told a story, and she told it with such feeling and passion, it made you feel it too. That day in April she sang her entire Hot Cha's repertoire: "Them There Eyes" and "When the Moon Turns Green." When she finished, it was like summer thunder—one of the most resounding ovations I ever heard. People were begging for more. But Billie walked offstage, and I went out to settle the crowd. I said, "Folks, what can I say? She only rehearsed the two numbers. Those two songs are all she can do right now. Come back tomorrow and she'll have rehearsed another two songs and you can hear all four."

Nobody wanted to hear that talk. They kept on stomping and clapping and hollering, and I looked over at Billie and she was grinning like it was the happiest day of her life. She was just beaming. She couldn't believe that applause. I could have told her it was the sound of a great career taking off. I was getting ready to announce the next act when a voice boomed through all the noise. It must have been someone in the last row of the last balcony with a bellow to rival Paul Robeson's. "Let her sing 'em again, Coop," the man said. And the audience took up the line in rhythm, "Sing 'em again! Sing 'em again!" So Billie Holiday came back out and poured her heart into those same two songs. Everyone listened, hushed and reverent, and when she finished, it was thunder all over again.

In those days, we never booked an act for more than a week at a time. But Billie stayed for four weeks straight, four shows a day. And each week she moved one step up, until by the end of the month she was the headlining star.

Billie was from a small-time show-business family. Her father was Clarence Holiday, who used to play guitar for Fletcher Henderson's big band. She was born in Baltimore, but she grew up in Harlem. After the Apollo shows, she toured with Teddy Wilson's band as well as Artie Shaw's and Count Basie's; she even led her own band for a while. But Billie's legend was born downtown on Swing Street. Billie became a huge draw in the best clubs on 52nd Street, which was the scene for big-time jazz in the 1940s. Swing Street was as close as downtown came to Harlem's 133rd Street. It was where the action was, and Billie was the queen of the scene. She didn't have fans—she had worshippers. When she finished her nine o'clock show, she would go check out the acts at the other nightspots that lined the street. But back at her club, where they wouldn't see Billie again until after midnight, nobody would move. Those were high-paying audiences, but they would sit there and drink up the booze and smoke up the pot and wait. Finally someone would see her coming up the block, and they'd bring her stool out and set it up under the spotlight in the middle of the floor. That was the signal that Billie was on her way. She would walk in, lazily drop her coat on the floor, stroll over, perch on that stool, and start snapping her fingers. Then she would sing.

What an amazing artist—and a helluva personality. Billie had two feisty little Chihuahuas she always took around with her. They'd attack you in a minute. I'd put my hand down to pet them and they would bite. Billie would say, "Shame on you for biting the nice man." Then she would say, "Here, Ralph, let me wrap that for you." And she would take her silk handkerchief and wrap my hand with it. She was a lovely woman and a tragic person. Like so many of the greats, she couldn't manage life without the powder, the heroin. The same thing that made her such a beautiful, sensitive singer made her vulnerable and scared. She thought she needed the drug to protect her and keep her safe. And it killed her.

I'm just proud that the Apollo was the place that first projected her to stardom.

As our Amateur Night audience grew each week, Morris Sussman began buying more and more space to advertise the show and its master of ceremonies. "Every Wednesday, 11 p.m. to Midnight. Broadcast Direct From Stage—WMCA Amateur Night in Harlem with the Inimitable RALPH COOPER—Listen In!" The columnists ladled out praise for "Ralph Cooper, emcee par excellence." V. E. Johns devoted an entire column to the Apollo's surprise success. "To Ralph Cooper belongs much of the credit," Johns wrote.

> Cooper joined the Apollo staff a year ago as master of ceremonies and today he is found on the Apollo stage doing a magnificent job.
>
> The Cooper personality infects both the audience and the performers. His bubbling natural humor keeps the audience happy and spurs the entertainers on to their best, and his versatility enables him to thread the show together and make it run smoothly and swiftly.
>
> It is this Cooper personality that is being felt over the air waves and radio listeners are catching the spirit. This broadcast must mean much to the Apollo and it means a great deal to Harlem too. It is putting Harlem on the map and spreading the knowledge and realization of Harlem, or, I should say, colored, talent.

Whew! I loved reading that column fifty years ago, and it still reads darn well, in my opinion.

But the highest praise I ever received came from the kids who used to hang out in the 126th Street alley by the backstage door. These kids would wait back there for me to arrive so they could hit me up for free passes. The theatre always had a dozen or so passes available for each show. To be validated, the passes had to be signed by one of the theatre managers or producers. So when kids asked me for passes and there were some available, I'd sign over a couple for them. This went on for months, until one day I happened to walk out to the box office and one of the alley urchins I had just given a pass to was there buying a ticket to the show. "Why are you buying a ticket when I just gave you a free one?" I said.

"Oh, Mr. Cooper," the kid said. "We never use those passes."

"Why not?"

"We save them."

I was incredulous. "Well, why do you save them?"

"For your autograph" was the reply.

That made me feel pretty good.

But then I got brought down a notch when a local restaurant started naming menu items after celebrities. The Mills Brothers had the high-price, one-dollar chicken platter, and Don Redman rated a forty-cent plate of lamb chops. So I felt somewhat slighted when I glanced down the menu and saw the Ralph Cooper liver-and-onions special priced at a measly two bits.

By the end of our first year, the Apollo was so closely associated with the weekly Wednesday festivities that when burglars jimmied a skylight on the roof of the theatre and made off with seven hundred dollars' worth of band equipment and tuxedos from Lucky Millinder's orchestra, the papers referred to the Apollo as "the home of Amateur Night in Harlem." (The instruments were later recovered in Harlem pawn shops, and cops from the 135th Street precinct collared the perpetrators six weeks after the robbery when someone reported seeing a teenager walking down Seventh Avenue in the middle of the afternoon wearing one of the hot—and expensive—evening jackets.)

When we first opened, Morris Sussman started booking groups like Lil Armstrong, who was best known because she was Louis's wife. But once the radio broadcasts began, he was able to book the superstars, because he could promise them national radio exposure during the Harlem Amateur Night show.

Louis Armstrong was one of the most famous names in show business in the 1930s. Whenever Louis played the Apollo, the theatre would have the most wonderful scent. At first I couldn't figure out what it was. It was almost like a perfume in the air. I would announce Louis, and two seconds later there was a sweet cloud over the theatre. Finally I realized that everybody was lighting their pot up to dig Pops.

A new music was born right around the time the Apollo opened. It was big-band swing, a music form that soon became a national craze. But in the mid-thirties, swing was a rhythmic innovation developed by Fletcher "The King of Swing" Henderson, one of the great orchestra leaders, whose style influenced all the bands in Harlem. Swing became so big uptown, Harlem became known as "Swing Pan Alley." It was only much later that swing caught on among the white orchestra leaders like the Dorsey brothers and Benny Goodman. When Goodman became world famous as the King of Swing himself, Harlem jazz lovers knew he was a pretender to the throne, because Goodman had hired the real king, Fletcher Henderson, to create his early arrangements!

Until we started broadcasting over WMCA, most people outside of Harlem and Chicago, and a few other cities where black musicians thrived, didn't know a thing about swing. But they heard plenty of it once they tuned in to our amateur hour and heard the headliners. We gave the sound and some of the bands that blew it—Lionel Hampton and Earl "Fatha" Hines and Don Redman—their first national exposure.

Hard as they are to find, most histories written about black show business in Harlem, and the Apollo in particular, tell it like it wasn't. They ignore the people who really accomplished something, and in many cases give all the credit to people for things they had nothing to do with. But the historians are correct to conclude that the WMCA live broadcasts of my show gave the mass white audience its first exposure to "the new sounds of black swing music."

Before swing became popular around the world, the new music became the center of a storm of controversy. For years there had been an ongoing war in the newspapers between progressive and conservative pundits over the intellectual and creative abilities of black Americans. Throughout the Jazz Age and the Swing Era that followed, the debate centered on black music and whether or not it was art or some primitive black magic that threatened to turn America into a nation of sex-addled, dope-smoking, beat-crazy jazz fiends.

There was a sense of real urgency about the debate in the 1930s, when racial injustice was law and those few liberals who spoke out in favor of racial equality were often branded as communists. Sub-

God's eye may have been on the sparrow, but our eyes were all on Ethel Waters, who was a member of the Apollo Theatre family long before she became world famous for her role in *The Member of the Wedding.*

scribers to any of the eight major black newspapers that circulated in Harlem in the 1930s—the New York *Age,* the *Amsterdam News,* the *Afro-American,* the New York *Journal and Guide,* the Chicago *Defender,* the Pittsburgh *Courier, The Tattler* and *The Voice* read daily front-page reports of lynchings in "the South," the suppression and slaughter of innocents by American Marines in the black republic of Haiti, and the coming to absolute power of a racist government in Germany, where once welcome expatriate black Americans were being rounded up and deported. When Ethel Waters sang on national radio, white newspaper editors throughout the South protested. When Will Rogers used the word "nigger" in his radio show and Tom Mix commented that lynching was sometimes necessary in order to maintain law and order, black editors advocated boycotts of Rogers's sponsors and Tom Mix movies. Black intellectuals complained that songs like "Ol' Man River" and other show tunes written by whites were demeaning because they used stereotypes of black dialect and behavior.

Not all whites were reactionary. The conductor Leopold Stokowski and composer Dmitry Shostakovich issued public statements declaring Duke Ellington the world's greatest living composer, period. And famed Swiss psychologist Carl Gustav Jung said that blacks, once an enslaved race, "now rule whites spiritually through their music."

And not all black intellectuals held progressive views. The *Journal and Guide* weighed in with the opinion that jazz was not art. "The Negro race has been acclaimed for its gifts of special rhythm and peculiar idioms to music," an editorial said. "But most often, the Negro's crude musical lore has been refined into grander compositions by more serious white composers." Roll over, Stokowski, and tell Shostakovich the news. Even the once respected black historian and Howard University professor Carter G. Woodson, editor and founder of *Journal of Negro History,* declaimed in a widely circulated column that black, African-based rhythms were working evil wonders in America. "Syncopation," the professor wrote, "has done more to retard the [black] race than anything else." He went on to suggest that blacks should "concentrate on more lofty types of music" than jazz.

But Woodson really blew all credibility when he gushed praise for that champion of the downtrodden Adolf Hitler. One of Hitler's first acts upon taking power in 1933 was to forbid all "race-mixing" jazz concerts and to order the deportation of all blacks from German soil. It was part of Hitler's plan to wipe out all his opposition among the intelligentsia. So it was a shock to read that a leading black intellectual believed "Hitler set a noble example." "Would to God," Woodson wrote, "that [Hitler] had the power not to drive them from one country to another, but to round up all jazz promoters and performers of both races in Europe and America and execute them as criminals."

In the end, of course, the debate was won in the most eloquent way by the musicians, black and white, who made certain that jazz not only survived and thrived with swing and bebop but lived on in

A fur coat…

…and a Packard touring auto—trappings of my first success.

all its modern offspring, including rhythm and blues, rock and roll, soul, and funk. But back in 1934, black culture was just making itself seen and heard in America. And nowhere was a louder ruckus being raised than at the Apollo Theatre, which in just one short year had already established itself as black America's cultural capital.

Unfortunately, the Apollo had become *too* successful for my own good. In the spring of 1935, my feeling of euphoria ended abruptly when my old nemesis from the Lafayette Theatre, Frank Schiffman, took over as general manager and co-owner of the Apollo. The Apollo had proved to be the one competitor Frank Schiffman couldn't beat— so he joined instead.

5

The Theatrical Battle for Harlem

★ ★

HOW TO LOSE (BLACK) FACE AND GAIN RESPECT

In June 1934, six months after the Apollo's first serving of "Jazz A La Carte," theatrical warlord Leo Brecker and his field general, manager Frank Schiffman, opened a new front in the Harlem theatre wars—the Harlem Opera House on 125th Street.

For six months, we'd been beating up on the Lafayette, which had fallen on hard times since the Apollo opened. Brecker and Schiffman had already put the Lafayette on rations, reducing prices and cutting back on production costs to the extent that the newspaper reviewers took to ridiculing the once grand theatre for putting on mediocre entertainments that were an insult to "the scattered few" in attendance. By the time the Harlem Opera House opened, the Lafayette had been forced into an embarrassing retreat. Following the lead of Harlem's other now-dark vaudeville houses—the Alhambra, the Lincoln, and the Renaissance—the fabled Lafayette Theatre, once the premier show palace of black entertainment, became a drafty movie theatre, showing double features to sparse audiences of lonely men and women who had to huddle in their overcoats because management had turned down the heat in the vast auditorium to save money.

Located just a half block from the Apollo, the Harlem Opera House was part of Brecker and Schiffman's strategy to bring the battle for Harlem to our doorstep. But try as they might, the Harlem Opera House never equaled the Apollo in the quality of its stage productions or acceptance by the public, which never got in the habit of taking in its shows. Everyone in town knew what Schiffman was up to. The Harlem Opera House was such an imitator of the Apollo, it became known as the Little Tent and we were the Big Tent. Both theatres were determined that it would be the other tent that would be forced to fold.

Schiffman tried to copy everything we did, from our revue format and comedy bits to our newspaper ad designs. We had a reverse white on black logo at the top of our ads with our address and slogans "America's Smartest Colored Shows!" and "Biggest Shows at the Lowest Prices" written in the O's of the word "APOLLO."

So Schiffman put circles at the top of his ads, with matching slogans: "Greatest Show Value in Harlem" and "America's Leading Colored Theatre." Schiffman tried to compensate for weak, poorly conceived stage productions by booking big-name, high-priced talent, including Jimmie Lunceford, Cab Calloway, Earl Hines, and Duke Ellington. I often imagined I could hear Frank Schiffman cursing the Harlem Opera House's budget-busting bookings all the way up in my dressing room at the Apollo, a half-block away.

Just how desperate Schiffman was became clear to me when he and his associates made me an offer I was happy to refuse. Schiffman and the other theatre managers from Philadelphia, Baltimore, and Washington who operated what we called the Round the World circuit called me to a meeting at the Harlem Opera House, where Schiffman was making his last stand in his war with the Apollo. The group had a proposition for me. They would pay me considerably more money than I was making at the Apollo if I would quit and come to work for them as a producer putting shows together for the circuit. It was a tempting offer, but I didn't give it more than a second's thought before I turned them down flat. I was happy at the Apollo, and I wouldn't have gone voluntarily to work for Frank Schiffman for a million dollars. Despite what would transpire in a few short months, I never regretted my decision.

Whenever I read in the papers about contract skirmishes between talent and management at the Harlem Opera House, I would breathe a sigh of relief and remind myself how lucky I was to be above the endless fray at the Schiffman camp.

At first, Schiffman's artillery seemed weak. It certainly wasn't much of a threat when he started a "Tuesday Amateur Night" at the Harlem Opera House to counter my big Wednesday-night gun. But I did think he was going too far when, after seeing how successful our arrangement with WMCA was, he started broadcasting his Tuesday show over WNEW. He even had the nerve to call his show "Amateur Night in Harlem"—which was my show's title. Ultimately, it reposed in potter's field.

I knew a lot of people who hated Frank Schiffman, and the Apollo's owner, Sid Cohen, was one of them. He always used to say how much he loathed the imperious way Schiffman dealt with the people around him, especially the blacks who worked for him. From the janitors in the basement to the stars on his stage, Frank Schiffman disdained them all. I'll never forget that spring day in 1935 when negotiations for the theatre were concluded. That was the day Sid Cohen died suddenly. Not only was it a sad and disastrous day for black performers, it was quite a personal setback for me. Sid had just spoken to me about signing a contract that would guarantee me a bonus appreciation of one hundred dollars per week (equal now to about five hundred dollars) as long as the Apollo was open, regardless of ownership. Sid said he wanted to devote himself to his real estate business. He was going to turn all management duties over to Morris Sussman. It was as if Sid knew something was going to happen. He was putting his house in order. I was on my way to his office downtown to sign the agreement that he had offered in appreciation of my work and help. When I got there, I was told Sid had just dropped dead from a heart attack in the building's barber shop.

From then on, the news just got worse. Morris Sussman, who was also Sid's business partner as well as his general manager, surrendered to Sid's worst enemy. I'll never understand why he did it, but management signed a contract agreeing to sell the Apollo outright to Schiffman's boss, Leo Brecker, who in turn gave his victorious general, Schiffman, an interest in the spoils. On May 15, 1935, formal announcement of the deal was made. Backstage at the Apollo we called it "the devil's pact." The papers called it a "merger" of the Apollo and the Harlem Opera House, which was immediately turned into a movie theatre.

One of the first things Schiffman did when he took over was to change the Apollo's ad copy to read "The Only Stage Show in Harlem.'' For Schiffman, that said it all. He had won the battle and the war. Where once there had been half a dozen black vaudeville theatres in Harlem, there was but one. But Schiffman didn't care, because he owned it.

Officially, Morris Sussman had some say in the Apollo's management. But in practice, it was Schiffman's theatre, to do with as he pleased. Schiffman's lifelong dream had come true. He had vanquished all his enemies. The kill had been made for him. Now he was alone to enjoy the feast.

According to all the scuttlebutt, this turn of events did not bode well for me. While most of the newspapers reserved judgment on whether or not the ''merger'' was good for Harlem show business, Lou Layne hinted that it was not when he reported in the *Age* the insider gossip that ''one of Frank Schiffman's first official acts under the joint managerial policy will be, of all things, to fire Ralph Cooper!'' Luckily, WMCA had something to say about that. And though my days at the Apollo were numbered, Schiffman found that as much as he might want to—it had been less than two years since I told him what to do with his blacklist—it wasn't going to be easy to get rid of the Amateur Night creator, the man the papers called ''Harlem's own son'' and ''the idol of Harlem.'' Both the theatre and the radio station were besieged by callers protesting Schiffman's plan to dump me. All I can surmise is that Morris Sussman must have intervened on my behalf, because I doubt any number of mere Harlemites would have been enough to sway Schiffman.

In the end my boosters prevailed, and the *Amsterdam News* put the word out. '' 'Amateur Night in Harlem' with Ralph Cooper as master of ceremonies,'' the paper reported, ''will continue to be broadcast direct from the stage of the 125th Street Apollo theatre at eleven every Wednesday night, the management disclosed after numerous inquiries. Radio station WMCA will continue to carry the broadcast from the stage.''

Like all conquerors, Schiffman knew it was in his best interest to sit back and consolidate his power. He would deal with renegade heroes later—or so he thought.

From that time forward, my working relationship with Schiffman was strained at best. But because we had to continue working together, we worked out a kind of détente where I kept out of his way and he kept out of mine. And despite all the backstage tension that Schiffman brought with him, I still remember those first years of the Apollo as among the best of my life.

That spring, my Amateur Night show was ranked as a New York City "High Spot" in the annual poll published by the New York *Daily News*. The show continued to give big boosts to some local talents, including a "snake hips" dancer named Herman Smith; a young Harlem girl singer named Pauline Edwards, who got rave reviews when we put her on for a week's run; a "reformed" Alabama schoolteacher named Ethel Harper; and a Harlem girl named Carolyn Wright, who the papers said "swings along better than some of the professionals on the bill."

I remember one very talented amateur who lost in a big way. He was white and sounded like Paul Robeson, with a rich, booming, beautiful baritone voice. But he made an unfortunate choice of material. He wanted to sing "Ol' Man River." As written, by a white lyricist (Oscar Hammerstein II), the opening verse of that now standard song has the line "Niggers all work on de Mississippi." When Paul Robeson and other black singers sang "Ol' Man River," they generally substituted "darkies" or "colored folk"—anything but "niggers." Sometimes they simply deleted the verse. But this fellow was a purist, and he wanted to sing the song as it was written, which wasn't the brightest thing in the world to do. So he started singing "Ol' Man River," and immediately dropped his bomb: "Niggers all work on de Mississippi." No explosion could have been as loud as the silence that followed. But people figured they heard wrong, and the man kept on singing. He thought he sounded fine and went on to the next line: "Niggers all work while de white folks play." Now the audience knew they heard right, and all hell broke loose. The boos were deafening. I gave the man the siren, and Porto Rico ran out to give him the bum's rush. It was too bad—he had a nice voice. But if his brains had been dynamite they wouldn't have blown his hat off.

Speaking of "Ol' Man River," that was one of the most popular songs among our amateur singers. I couldn't guess how many contestants sang that number; it was performed so often it became a joke. One day Tiny Bradshaw, the bandleader, told me he knew "Ol' Man River" so well and had heard it so many times, he was going to sing it backwards. I thought that was a great idea, so I hyped it up in the theatre. For a week before Tiny's engagement, I told every audience about his proposition. "Next week when Tiny headlines, he's going to sing 'Ol' Man River' and he's going to sing it backwards. So tell everybody. Tiny Bradshaw's going to be in here next week and he's going to sing everybody's favorite song, 'Ol' Man River,' backwards." I really built up expectations for Tiny. So when he came in I told him, "Okay, baby, I got 'em ready for you."

Tiny came on and did his set. Then he said, "Ladies and gentlemen, I'm going to do something for you that's never been done. I'm going to sing 'Ol' Man River' backwards." Everybody applauded, whistled, stamped their feet. Tiny's band hit the intro for "Ol' Man River"—and that fool turned around and put his back to the audience and sang "Ol' Man River, dat Ol' Man River . . . he jes' keeps rollin'. . . ."

People died. It was a great gag. To this day I can't believe I fell for it—didn't even see it coming.

Amateur Night in Harlem continued to sell out every Wednesday, and the radio show remained the number-one show for its time slot week after week. So many talented kids showed up each week to test their talent and nerve that one Saturday we staged a marathon show featuring two hundred Harlem amateurs.

Despite Schiffman's takeover, my star continued to rise. The *Age* declared that I was "undoubtedly the outstanding master of ceremony on the sepia stage." And the Pittsburgh *Courier* ran a full-page feature about me under the banner headline RALPH COOPER SENSATIONAL! Of course I couldn't have agreed with them more. I was truly touched by the *Courier*'s Billy Rowe, who wrote that "on Amateur Nights, Cooper has a way of making the amateur feel happy if he succeeds and not feel bad if he does not succeed. The man even throws bricks gracefully. Ralph has carved himself a niche in the hearts of the Apollo public that is as indestructible as the need and urge for entertainment itself."

"Yes indeedy," as I used to say onstage.

Even Schiffman recognized a hot property when he saw one, and booked me and my old band the Kongo Knights for a week's engagement at the Apollo. During the Amateur Night radio broadcast that week, I found myself acting as master of ceremonies as well as headline attraction. It was a gas to lead an orchestra again, and the audiences seemed to enjoy it as much as I did. The *Daily News* review

Very young, very lovely, very gifted, Pearl Bailey was an Amateur Night winner. Her brother Bill, one of the finest tap dancers in the land, died tragically from a drug overdose before he was able to fulfill his enormous promise.

noted that "Ralph Cooper, in addition to his emcee duties, tries a bit of serious crooning and dancing and does well at both."

Knowing I couldn't keep on running the amateur show single-handed, I began to audition substitute emcees. But none of the people I tried worked out until I found Willie Bryant, who was a popular Harlem bandleader. Willie had just the right kind of charisma and good-humored stage style to do the job, and he eventually became one of the Apollo's best-loved Amateur Night emcees.

Lionel Hampton's acrobatic percussion work was a frequent and featured attraction at the Apollo.

Radio not only made the Apollo Theatre world famous, it also made a star of our audience. I used to say that the stars of our Wednesday-night shows are amateurs, but the fifteen hundred audience members who show up every week are pros. Lionel Hampton liked to tell reporters in the 1930s that so many people in the audience got to stomping and jumping one night while he was playing ''Flyin' Home,'' he was sure the upper balcony was going to crack and send the wild ones upstairs spilling into the laps of the people in the orchestra seats below. Earl "Fatha" Hines wrote one of his big hits, "Second Balcony Jump," about the Apollo audience.

Upstairs, the aisles are steep and short and the railings are low. One night Earl was playing and a fella got excited and ran the length of the center aisle in the top balcony. When he reached the rail, he just kept going. He flipped right over the rail, and he would have dropped straight into the orchestra seats below if somebody in the rail row hadn't caught him by the ankle and held on. The flyer hung there, dangling head-first from the top rail. Something about the way the crowd below was staring up at him must have sobered him up, because he looked like he'd seen his own ghost. Finally, a couple of the catcher's neighbors pitched in and hauled the flyer back to safety. Everybody in the theatre stood up and gave him an ovation—and Earl Hines had himself a hit song, "Second Balcony Jump."

Sammy Davis, Jr., knew how tough the Apollo audience could be. Sammy grew up on 140th Street in Harlem, and his mother, Baby Sanchez, still lives in Harlem. For a short time she worked as a dancer in the Apollo chorus line, so Sammy felt right at home in the Apollo— or at least he should have. When he started out, Sammy was no more than Michael Jackson's age. Even as a little boy of five, Sammy was a sensation in his miniature black suit and top hat and tiny dancing feet working with the Will Mastin Trio. All the old hoofers I knew assumed Sammy was going to be the next generation's greatest tap dancer. Actually, he became one of the greatest entertainers.

When Sammy was in his teens, he returned to the Apollo as the trio's star attraction. Besides dance and tap, he was singing now and doing impressions. He'd been doing this new act for over a year; he had performed in all the biggest theatres in the country, and he knew his material cold. But when he got to the Apollo, he was struck with fear. When he got out there and the spotlight was on him and he looked up at the theatre full of people all cheering and clapping and whistling for him, he just clammed up. He opened his mouth and nothing came out—not a word. He was struck dumb. Later, he said the audience "scared the voice right out of me." That only increased the audience's legend. And it made it twice as tough on young amateurs. They had to think, "If that audience scared Sammy Davis, Jr., so bad, what are they gonna do to me? They won't even bother chewing me up. They'll just swallow me whole."

Performance is a wonderful thing. It takes you into another world. It gives you an opportunity to sing, move, let your feelings go. It's like a shot of adrenaline. There's just nothing like that jolt. Live performance makes you feel alive. But it's also a naked, vulnerable, and intimate feeling. Kids get out there and their hearts beat different. It can be a very frightening thing to do.

Sometimes I wish the audience wouldn't be so cruel. But then I remember that if a kid wants to be a star, there is one sure way to find out if he's got what it takes. And he doesn't have to take an aptitude test or solicit the opinions of experts. All he has to do is get out there in front of the jury of fifteen hundred, put the needle in the groove, and move. He'll find out quick enough if he's got the thing.

One of the contributions I'm most proud of from my early years at the Apollo is the role I played in helping to end the use of blackface at the theatre.

Many of the comics I worked with in those days were accustomed to wearing burnt cork to darken their faces, as well as big white grease lips, a nappy wig, and white gloves. Blackface was a holdover from minstrel shows and the so-called pickaninny players. Later, when blacks first began to appear on Broadway and in the movies, they were required to wear blackface. Apparently, whites felt more comfortable around blacks if they were in blackface. That way they could feel superior.

Al Jolson, who was the biggest star of his day, carried the idea of a white man covering black material to an extreme. Jolson never appeared without his nappy wig and blackface and big white lips. And vaudeville's Amos and Andy were white men Freeman Gosden and Charles Correll in blackface who had the biggest hit radio show in the country. Eddie Cantor and Georgie Jessel were other top white comics who wore blackface. And, like Jolson, they copied the antics, movements, and dances of black show people; they sang songs by black composers in the style of black blues artists. And it wasn't just the men. Let's not forget that Sophie Tucker climbed to stardom with her rendition of "Some of These Days," written by Shelton Brooks, a black comic who emulated the great Bert Williams. So I can only assume that Jolson and the rest were emulating the black comics, not making fun of them.

It's hard to imagine the great stars of today wearing blackface.

"Here come da Judge!" Pigmeat Markham and I wrote that line together, but Pig made it all his own. The creator of the Truck, the dance craze that swept Jazz Age America, Pigmeat became the Apollo's leading comedy star after I brought him to the Apollo when the theatre first opened. As enormous as his talent was, Pig was still wearing burnt-cork blackface makeup when this photo was taken during one of our skits at the Apollo. But at my urging, Pig soon quit wearing the cork.

Eddie Murphy might do it as a joke—Ben Vereen did. But can you dig James Brown singing "Say It Loud—I'm Black and I'm Proud" in cork? It would be absurd. Yet one of the greatest black comics I ever knew wore cork when it was acceptable.

Pigmeat Markham's real name was Dewey Markham. Somehow, "Dewey" just doesn't fit him. In the old days, all black comics had a handle of some kind. They were never known as Eddie or Richard. They had names like Dusty, Apus, Crackshot, Onions, Ashes and Bilo, Pigmeat, Dr. Sausage or Bear.

I brought Pig to the Apollo from a Forty-second Street burlesque house, where he used to work with his partner, Johnny Leelong. Pig and Johnny were doing a midnight show when Pigmeat came upstairs to tell Johnny to get ready. It was time for them to go on. Johnny was bent over the dressing table sound asleep with his head down. Pigmeat nudged him gently on the arm and said, "C'mon, man, we gotta go on." But Johnny Leelong didn't wake up. Instead, he rolled right off the chair and hit the floor, dead.

Pigmeat just broke down on the spot. He was inconsolable for weeks. I told Pig he had to go on with his own life, but he said he missed Johnny Leelong too much and he didn't want to work without him. I eventually talked him into coming up to the Apollo, and I talked Sussman into hiring him.

At that time, Pig still wore cork. I believed in his talent, but I thought it was demeaning for him to wear it. Of course I wasn't alone in hating cork. My old pal Vere E. Johns said that blackface appealed only to "yokels, morons and nincompoops" and was a practice popular only among "antiquated baboons of a bygone and ignorant age [who] should be cremated." I never had the heart to show Pig those reviews. But one day I saw him run in through the backstage door, late for a show. He headed upstairs to rub on the cork, and I stopped him. "Wait a minute, Pig," I said.

"Coop—I'm late. I'll talk to you after. I gotta get my face on."

"Forget the cork today, Pig," I said. "Your own face is fine."

Pig looked at me like I was Abe Lincoln. "Yeah, man," he said. "Forget the cork." Pig never wore the cork again.

Most of the comedy we did in those days was situation comedy. There were no stand-up comics in those days. We did quick sketches we called "bits" or "blackouts," which meant that after the punch line, the spots go out and the stage would be dark, blacked out, for a second. Then the lights would flash on and the show would continue. "Rowan and Martin's Laugh-In" in the sixties used a modified blackout technique for their one-liners. That show also picked up one of our most famous routines, "Here Come da Judge." Pigmeat became famous for that routine, written by yours truly. It evolved from a routine in which the bailiff called the court to order: with a drumbeat and a rap-style narrative that preceded L.L. Cool J by fifty years:

> Hear ye, hear ye the Court of Swing
> Is now about ready to do its thing.
> Don't want no tears, don't want no jive,
> Above all things, don't want no lies.
> Our judge is hip, his boots are tall

He'll judge you Jack, big or small.
So fall in line, his stuff is sweet,
Peace, brothers, here's Judge Pigmeat!

The band would go into a riff and Pigmeat would make his entrance, truckin' in his robe and graduation cap with everybody hollering in tempo, ''Here come da Judge! Here come da Judge!''

Pigmeat would get up on the judge's bench, pound an enormous gavel onto the Manhattan phone book, and call the court into session. ''The Judge is mean this mornin','' he'd say. ''I'm going to open court by giving myself thirty days, next case.'' And then a short little policeman would come in wearing a funny-looking uniform. It was all a satire on the police and the courts, and audiences always loved that.

The first case would be a gorgeous girl the cop picked up on 114th Street at three o'clock in the morning. Pig would say, ''What you doin' out at three o'clock in the mornin', honey?''

''I'm a beautician,'' she would say, fluttering her lashes and swinging her hips. ''One of my clients was leaving town early in the morning, and I had to do her hair.''

Then Pig would turn on the cop. ''What's the matter with you, pickin' up somebody like this? This child is a workin' child. Case dismissed!'' Then he'd lean over the bench, his eyebrows dancing and his tongue wagging, and he'd say to the girl, ''Have I got your name and phone number, honey?''

Then there would be a drum shot—BAM!—and the last defendant would enter—me, in drag. I would have two big helium balloons for breasts, and I'd be pulling at my sweater and they'd bounce up in the judge's face. The critics would wince, but the audience would fall out over that every time. Pigmeat would pound his gavel for order in the court and he'd look me over and say, ''What are you doing in my courtroom? What is your crime?''

''Oh, Judge,'' I'd say, ''I was streetwalkin', Your Honor!''

''Say what?''

''I said I was streetwalkin', Judge, Your Honor.''

''You make your livin' that way?''

''I could, Your Honor, if it weren't for those damn beauticians!''
Drum shot. Blackout.

In another situation, we had Pig at the doctor's office. A nurse would tell him to get undressed, and he'd hesitate, waiting for her to leave. "What are you waitin' for?" she'd say.

"Well, I got to get undressed. I've got to take my clothes off."

"Well, go right ahead," the nurse would say. "Those little things don't bother me." BOOM! Blackout.

Steve Miller, the carpenter, created some wonderful sets for our comedy routines. Our "Here Come da Judge" set was like a cartoon drawing of a courtroom. For another routine, he built a big double-decker bus that could roll from one end of the stage to the other. Jimmy Baskett would play the driver, and Pig and I would be the only passengers. We'd ride up on top as the double-decker rolled through town, and I would majestically wave and greet all passersby. I'd be all friendly and nice. "Hey, man," I'd say, "ain't that Clarence down there? Hi, Clarence. Lookin' good, man! Yeah!" Then, as soon as the bus rolled by, I'd stab him: "What that jive Clarence—he acts like he's got something. He ain't got enough money to buy a bandage for six mosquitoes."

Critical old Mr. Johns hated bits like that. "Reminded me of the days when Hurtig and Seamon had the house. Burlesque, you know," he would sniff. But the audiences loved those routines and the Apollo became known as much for its comedy as for its musical entertainment.

Not everyone at the theatre reaped the rewards of the Apollo's success. The Apollo chorus line directed by Clarence Robinson was widely regarded as the best in the city, uptown or downtown. Beautiful and talented ladies all, the dancers had to work exhausting hours, seven days a week, four shows a day, with five on Sunday and a Saturday midnight show, plus at least one night of rehearsals for the following week's show. It was a murderous schedule, and the dancers were working for slave wages. Each dancer was paid thirty-five dollars a week for twenty-nine shows plus rehearsals.

In 1935, Clarence Robinson, who was responsible for distributing the girls' pay envelopes, went on a month-long vacation to Europe. Before he left, he asked me to take care of the payroll for the Rockettes. The first week I did it, the girls came in, signed for their pay, and I handed them their envelopes. But as each one opened her envelope, she would lean over and give me a hug and a kiss and say, "Thank you, Coop." I thought to myself, "No wonder this bum

In the late thirties, the Apollo chorus girls went on strike for higher wages. Here some of the dancers did a radio spot to earn a little extra cash. Within a few short years, the chorus was disbanded—and the great Apollo production numbers were ended—so Frank Schiffman could save a little money.

Clarence wants to pay the girls instead of the office. He gets a kiss every payday from sixteen sensuous, charming, beautiful ladies.'' It never dawned on me to ask the girls why all the kisses. I figured they just liked me. And besides, show people have a habit of being affectionate with one another. Anyhow, I didn't think much about it.

But later that afternoon, one of the dancers said to me, ''You know, Coop, that was real swingin' of you to get that raise for us.''

''What raise is that?'' I said.

''You know, the ten-dollar raise you got for us.''

I didn't know what she was talking about, but I said, ''Oh, sure. Don't mention it. You all certainly deserve it.''

That night I found out what the real story was. Clarence Robinson had been taking ten dollars from each pay envelope that actually was thirty-five dollars every week and pocketing it for himself. He'd been doing this for over a year, swiping a hundred and sixty dollars a week from these poor overworked dancers. Clarence (Clinker, we called him) was a lovable guy, and the dancers eventually forgave him—but not before they made sure someone else was responsible for their payroll.

One hot summer the chorus girls and I inadvertently invented a popular promotional stunt for the theatre. There was a swimming pool—the Lido Pool—on 146th Street right off Seventh Avenue. It was just a bit too far to be able to walk there for a swim between shows and still get back in time. But we had a three-pedal-type Model T Ford that I bought for fifteen dollars up in the Bronx to use in a comedy bit. We kept the car stored in the alley behind the theatre. It was sweltering in the theatre that summer, so I hatched the idea of driving the car up to the Lido after the first show. The chorus girls loved it, and they would all squeeze into their bathing suits and pile into the Model T, and up to the pool we'd go.

Every day it seemed we'd have such a great time up at the Lido, we'd have to rush back to the theatre in time for the afternoon show. Invariably, coming back from the pool, somewhere between 135th and 130th Street the damn car would stop. It would stall out in the middle of Seventh Avenue and we couldn't get it started. So the girls would all jump out and push the car back down to 126th Street. People would see this, and naturally they'd drop whatever they were doing and rush out to help these poor beauties push the car. It became a big event on hot summer days.

That same summer, we all got in the habit of going out for dinner at Ma Bacon's. She was a great cook who served meals in the basement of her brownstone, just up 126th Street from the theatre's backstage entrance. Everybody in the crew and cast along with the headliners would troop down to Ma Bacon's after the second show of the day. Ma Bacon would set out a great big pitcher of lemonade; the pitcher would be sweatin' it was so cold. And she'd pull a big pan of hot rolls right out of the oven. She'd set 'em out on the table with butter and jelly and say, "Just a few moments, dears, and I'll have all the rest of the fixins for you." The cooking always seemed to take forever, and I'd down a pitcher full of lemonade myself and a whole tray of biscuits before the meal came. When Ma Bacon finally set the food out, I'd have a few nibbles and feel filled up. Then we'd pay up and rush back to the theatre, and by the time we were halfway through the next show, we'd be so hungry we couldn't see. So I'd send down to Ma Bacon's for sandwiches. Then for supper I'd send down for another plate of food. This went on for months before the bell finally rang and I realized why eating at Ma Bacon's made me so hungry. I just couldn't leave those hot biscuits and that cold lemonade alone. The biscuits swelled me up and the lemonade filled me up. It was like blowing a balloon up in my stomach, so when the real food came I couldn't eat a thing.

At the end of 1936, we celebrated our great second year at the Apollo with a spectacular New Year's Eve show, starring the Empress of the Blues, Bessie Smith, as the headliner. When she came to New York for the show, she told the newspapers that she planned to retire— in 1960. I wish life had worked out that way for her. Bessie Smith was probably the greatest blues singer that ever lived.

In slave days, the blues were subversive. They were used by the slave laborers to pass along information. While the master thought "his children" were down by the levee just singin' and havin' themselves a fine old time, the black men and women were planning escape and rebellion. They were smiling and singing, all right. But if the owners had listened, they might have started to worry:

> We goin' down by the river
> We goin' be there about eight tonight
> We goin' down by the river
> Be sure to dress up right
> We goin' down by the river
> Gonna' ride underground rails tonight.

Bessie Smith was born in Tennessee, and she learned the blues from another great blues singer, Ma Rainey. The blues had been passed down from generation to generation, and by the time they reached Ma Rainey and Bessie Smith, people started to get rich off the blues. But it wasn't Bessie Smith or Ma Rainey or Mamie Smith, another great singer, who got rich.

The history of black show business in the twentieth century has been a history of rip-offs. Black artists have been getting burned on the business end of deals for generations. It certainly didn't begin with the rhythm-and-blues players of the 1950s, who never got paid for inventing rock and roll. Years before Ruth Brown sold millions of R&B records and ended up broke, the same thing happened to Ma Rainey, who never received one cent of royalties—not one cent. She recorded all her songs for a flat fee. When she would get back from a long tour, she'd ask for her royalty payments and the company would say there weren't any. They would haul out the big books and show her exactly where they spent her money: this much for the recording studio, this much for the band, this much for the tour bus, this much for hotels and clothes and big dinners. In the end there was nothing left for the artist who made it all happen to begin with. It was exactly the same thing that had happened to black sharecroppers in the South. They would work the land and make just enough money to stay alive and work it again next year. And they ended up not owning anything. The blues singers and almost all other black entertainers were victims of show business sharecropping.

One of the best—or worst—examples was Fats Waller. Fats was a genius, no question. He wrote so many great songs, I couldn't count them all. He would write a song one day and sell it the next day for fifty dollars or a bottle or two of gin. It's a tragedy when you think of how prolific and productive Fats Waller was and how he ended up with nothing but the fine silk suits they buried him in.

Bessie Smith sold two million records in 1924 alone—and that was when her career was just beginning. By 1930, she had sold over eight million records, but she didn't see much of that money. For her live shows she was the highest-paid black entertainer of her day. Her problem was she never had anyone help her figure out the business half of show business.

Bessie was a big, imposing woman. She had a reputation as a Mae West type because of songs like "Jellyroll," which was a funny tune chock-full of sexual innuendo: "I want some sugar for my bowl, a hot dog for my roll." Offstage, she wasn't bawdy at all. But she was very brusque and rough. Most of the old TOBA acts were like that. TOBA was the black vaudeville circuit—Theatrical Owners Booking Association. Performers called it Tough On Black Asses. Bessie spent her career playing in run-down dives, sleeping in seedy hotels or staying overnight in private homes in towns where Jim Crow kept blacks out of the hotels. For TOBA acts, there were no roadside accommodations, other than on the side of the road.

So that New Year's Eve at the Apollo was a triumph for Bessie Smith. She closed the show, which meant she was tops at the premier theatre in Harlem.

But it turned out to be the last time she ever played the Apollo. Bessie got in a big rumble with Schiffman that night about money she felt was owed her. When Frank tried to browbeat her into backing down, she bellowed right back at him. Not many people shouted at Frank Schiffman, for fear of losing their jobs. But Bessie really let him have it. She yelled louder than he did, and finally, with everybody watching, and wondering if she had gone too far, Bessie turned around and bent over and flipped her dress way up over her head and said in her big beautiful voice, "Frank Schiffman, come on over here and kiss my big black ass." Bessie had been ripped off all her life, and she wasn't going to take it anymore.

Two years before that, in 1933, Bessie made her last record for Columbia. I guess they had gotten all the money out of her they felt they could. After all the records she sold for them, they dropped her like a hot potato. And two years after that triumphant New Year's Apollo show, Bessie Smith died in a car wreck on her way to a performance in her home state of Tennessee. She was thirty-nine years old.

Many years later, I found out that Bessie died without enough money in the bank to pay for a headstone for her grave. Columbia Records didn't buy her one, and Frank Schiffman didn't buy her one. But it was fitting when, thirty-three years later, a white singer who idolized Bessie—Janis Joplin, another blues belter destined to die too young—bought a tombstone for Bessie's grave.

I'll always remember Bessie for what she said to Frank Schiffman. And it wasn't long before I had the chance to tell Schiffman the same thing.

It happened one night after a show when a couple of very well-dressed white men came backstage and asked if they could have a moment of my time. I said sure and invited them into my dressing room. As it turned out one of the men was Marvin Schenck, a producer representing the 20th Century–Fox studio in Hollywood. Schenck and his associate were, they said, involved in a film starring Shirley Temple called *Poor Little Rich Girl*. Bill Robinson, who was

To Mr. Cooper love Shirley Temple

When Bill "Bojangles" Robinson took sick in Hollywood, where he was choreographing Shirley Temple's *Poor Little Rich Girl*, the movie's producers flew to New York and asked me to go west to help finish the picture, which I still consider Shirley's best.

slated to be choreographer and act in the picture, had taken ill. Would I be interested in taking over? I was flattered, of course; but it would mean leaving the Apollo, temporarily at least, and moving to Los Angeles. After a lifetime in The City, that wasn't something I was anxious to do. I tussled with the decision for quite a while.

Later, on my way to Frank Schiffman's office, I thought about that day just two years before when I ran into him backstage at the Lafayette and asked him what he thought about the new theatre opening up on 125th Street. I also thought about how he had won the Harlem theatre war. And I realized that my leaving would make Schiffman's conquest of the Apollo complete. Yet, despite all I had done to make the Apollo a hit, with Schiffman as commander-in-chief I knew I would never rise in rank. No matter how much the audience liked me, I'd always be on Schiffman's list. I decided on my way to Schiffman's office that after helping so many young people reach for stardom, it was time I hoisted my own star.

I made the announcement as brief as possible. "Frank," I said, "your fondest dream has come true—I quit."

To my surprise, Schiffman tried to stop me. He threatened to hold me to my contract. But Schenck had assured me any contractual matters would be taken care of. He wasn't someone Schiffman could bully. Schiffman ran movie theatres. If he wanted Fox films, he'd do whatever they told him to do.

So I caught the first thing smoking and I ain't joking. I was gone before you could say, "Hollywood, here I come!"

Coop was on the way.

6

Dark Gable

★ ★

For show people, Hollywood exerts a pull as irresistible as Broadway. It is to performers what Jerusalem is to the tribes of Israel or Harlem is to African-Americans; it is a magnet, a Mecca, a holy calling.

So when I got the call, I had to heed it. Critics say *Poor Little Rich Girl,* with Alice Faye and Jack Haley, was Shirley Temple's best dance picture. And the producers apparently liked it too, because they offered me a five-year contract.

Later I was nicknamed "Dark Gable," but Hollywood wasn't really interested in a black leading man. When *Poor Little Rich Girl* wrapped, I hoped for acting work, but all the parts they offered me were Uncle Tom parts. "Yassuh" and "nosuh" dummy parts were all that was available for a young black actor in those days, even one with a studio contract. The stereotypes seem so offensive today; but in the 1930s, it was heresy to think that a black actor could do anything but play the devil or the dummy. Paul Robeson had the only real male roles in Hollywood films. And there were always occasions for black performers like Louis Armstrong and Fats Waller to play themselves. But the rest of the roles were stereotypes. If you didn't want to mug wide-eyed and scared and act the fool, there was no room for you in the big studios.

When I went out to Hollywood to do some choreography, I never dreamed that they would turn me into a movie star. This is what the studio called my "Dark Gable" look. Eddie Murphy, eat your heart out.

There was one actor who bent the system to work for him— Stepin Fetchit. Step acted on the screen and off the screen.

I got to know Step on the 20th Century–Fox studio lot, where he and Bill Robinson and I were their only black contract players. Fox, which was run by Darryl F. Zanuck, had an in-house film school where young performers and creative people could learn the movie business from top to bottom. I was enrolled in the school along with Jack Haley, Alice Faye, and Tyrone Power, who were all being groomed for stardom.

I decided that instead of appearing in pictures that demeaned blacks, I would try to *make* pictures that glorified blacks. Fox knew there was a market in the black community for films with stories about black people, starring black actors. However, they had no interest in their development. So they encouraged me in the studio school and taught me directing, scriptwriting, lighting, set designing—everything you needed to know about filmmaking.

The great Stepin Fetchit, a pal from my Hollywood days, joined me for a date at a Long Island nightclub in the forties. The other fellow with us is Sonny "Long Gone" Thompson, an exciting boogie piano player.

It was a great learning experience. And there were lots of laughs as well. I had a ball on the Fox lot.

And a big reason it was such a delightful experience was Step. He was a fabulous character. He would arrive at the studio every morning when on a shoot, in two Cadillacs. The first one carried his supply of near beer, which he drank like water all day long. Riding along with the near beer was his valet and his footman. Step rode to work in the second car. As soon as they pulled into the lot, Step's footman would jump out with a footstool and run to open the door of the second car for Step. Step's valet meanwhile would emerge from the first car carrying a gold hanger from which was draped the raggedy old costume Step would wear in that day's shoot. The footman would open the door for Step, and he would get out mumbling up a storm. "What are we doing here at seven o'clock in the morning?" he'd say. "I'll spend all morning sitting around doin' nothing until they call me to the shoot, and that won't be until the middle of the afternoon."

Every day, Step hit the floor fuming. And every day it was the same argument—why did the studio insist he arrive at seven when he wasn't going to be needed until two? The whole time I was there that was what happened every day. He'd arrive at seven and work at two. It was my guess that the studio did it on purpose, just for laughs in the morning.

Step hated telephones, and he refused to get one for the very reason the studio said he had to have one—so they could get in touch with him when they needed to. Finally the studio insisted and made it part of his contract that he have a telephone installed at his home. Step agreed, but Fox had to pay for it.

Darryl Zanuck was a very smart fellow, but he couldn't keep up with the subtle workings of Step's mind. Any time Zanuck wanted Step to do something, he would patiently explain to Step what was needed. Step would listen carefully, and when Zanuck was done, he'd say, "It sounds fine to me, Mr. Zanuck, but I'll have to talk it over with my manager, Mr. Goldberg, and get back to you." The next day, he would find Zanuck and tell him it was fine—Mr. Goldberg gave the go-ahead.

This happened on film after film until one day Zanuck wanted an immediate decision about something. "I'll have to consult with Mr. Goldberg first," Step said.

But Zanuck's patience had run out. "Look," he said, "give me Mr. Goldberg's number and I'll call him myself right now. I need an answer right now. I don't have time to wait for you to talk to him tonight and get back to me tomorrow. I'll talk to him personally. So please, give me his telephone number. I'm used to talking to managers. I can handle your Mr. Goldberg. Besides, I've been dealing with him through you for so long, it's about time I got to know him. What's his damn phone number?"

Zanuck had him. Step just smiled and shook his head and said, "Well, Mr. Zanuck, I guess you had to find out some day. *I'm* Mr. Goldberg."

So everyone realized the joke Step was running all that time. He was mocking the widely held assumption that behind every successful black man there had to be an all-powerful white figure, a manager or agent or banker who called all the shots and controlled the performer's life like he was a puppet. Step told me later that he did have managers and agents, but they worked for him, not the other way around. Stepin Fetchit played dummies all his life. After I got to know him, I realized what a great actor he really was. Actually, that was his downfall.

By the time my studies were complete, I was ready to make movies. Ultimately, I formed a production company, Million Dollar Productions, and I got to work. Enough happened to me in Hollywood to fill another book. But briefly, I spent about five years in Hollywood, and in that time I wrote and directed and starred in eight films.

Dark Manhattan was the first story penned by me. It was a gangster picture, and it became a huge hit in Harlem. I got a big kick out of hearing that when the movie was screened at the Apollo, it broke all attendance records back in my home theatre. Schiffman played the movie at the Apollo and at the Harlem Opera House at the same time. People naturally wanted to see it at the Apollo even though it cost more, because they got to see the stage show along with the film. So he oversold every performance at the Apollo, and when all seats were filled, he sent the extra ticket holders down to the Harlem Opera House. That's how they broke the all-time attendance record at the Apollo—by selling twice as many tickets as there were seats. Despite the fact that the contract called for the Apollo *only* and it was a flat buy not a percentage, what nobody knew was that Schiffman had only one print of the film. So as one reel ended at the Apollo, it was rewound by Doll Thomas, the projectionist, and rushed down to the Harlem Opera House, where it was played; and as soon as the second reel was screened at the Opera House, it had to be rewound again and rushed back to the Apollo in time for the second screening there.

My next movie script was another gangster film, called *Bargain with Bullets*. After that, I wrote, directed, and starred in my biggest

I lured Lena Horne (they dropped the final "e" in Hollywood) out of retirement to co-star in my first film—*The Duke Is Tops*, which I wrote and starred in. It was Lena's first picture too, but the studio liked her so much, they released it as "Lena Horn in *Bronze Venus*."

picture. It was a musical, and I thought for sure it was going to make me a big Hollywood star.

The Duke Is Tops had it all: action, romance, and a beautiful, talented leading lady—Lena Horne. I had known Lena since she was in the chorus line at the Cotton Club. But Lena had retired and had gone home to Pittsburgh with her husband and their new baby. Her father, Teddy Horne, was an entrepreneur who also lived in Pittsburgh. So it was like pulling teeth to convince Lena to come to Hollywood, even for the female lead in my picture. She was adamant about retirement. Only after hours of phone calls and help from mutual friends, including a columnist on the Pittsburgh *Courier,* did Lena finally accept my offer. At first there was some reluctance out west, because Lena's career was in eclipse, and not many people in Hollywood remembered her. But I knew she was a wonderful talent, and my conviction about her sold the producers.

So Lena came out to Hollywood and we made *The Duke Is Tops.* The cast, the shoot, and the finished product were all great. I was certain it would appeal to a broad audience of African-Americans, and I was right. The picture enjoyed sensational box office. The billing read "Ralph Cooper in *The Duke Is Tops,* with Lena Horne."

Then a funny thing happened. After we wrapped, Lena had been engaged to perform a vocal in an MGM musical that became an enormous hit. There were a total of nine hundred black theatres in the U.S. then, and our film played in about six hundred of them (at least three hundred were owned by competitors). There were, at the same time, some thirty-five thousand movie houses catering to white audiences in the U.S. Once that huge audience saw Lena in the MGM musical, she became a very hot Hollywood property. *The Duke Is Tops* was reissued with a change of title and new billing: "Lena Horne in the *Bronze Venus* with Ralph Cooper." There were no credits on the poster saying that Ralph Cooper wrote and directed the picture.

I never did hit the big time in Hollywood. I had to settle for the small type on the movie marquees. But I'm proud of the movies I made because they constituted the new cycle of blacks in modern-day portrayals. And I think that if things had been less prejudicial, it might have worked out for me in Hollywood. As it happened, it would be years before things really started to happen for blacks in the movies. Even today, years after Million Dollar Productions was in business, there still aren't many honest roles for black artists. However, Eddie Murphy has attained superstar status. There's an old saying in show business that whoever puts the most butts in the seats is regarded as a superstar. Eddie Murphy is the biggest box-office attraction in the movie business today.

By the time I returned to New York, entertainment had begun to undergo an enormous change. Movies and radio had changed the way people thought about show business.

The big bands were breaking up, and smaller combos were the new trend in music. Vaudeville houses were concentrating on motion

We called them "gorgeous gams" in those days. They belong to Theresa Harris, one of my costars in *Gangsters on the Loose* (*shown here*) and *Bargain With Bullets*.

pictures, and many of the great tap dancers, high-stepping chorus girls, and situation comics began looking for other lines of work. Most of the great clubs and all-night cafés Harlem was famous for were closed—133rd Street was dark. The Cotton Club remained open—some hundred blocks away, in the Times Square area downtown. Harlem's entertainment tradition can be compared to a beautiful sunny day that turns into a stormy night.

Even the look of the neighborhood had changed. Most of the big majestic trees were gone from the Boulevard of Dreams; the remaining ones had a shoddy unkempt appearance, and the clean, prosperous neighborhoods had begun to erode. The streets didn't seem as sparkling and full of promise as they once were. The beautiful brownstones and luxury apartment houses were looking old.

It was hard to fathom. Just a few years earlier, if someone had told me that the Apollo would be the last of the great Harlem theatres for live entertainment, that Mexico's and the Chicken Shack and the Madhouse would be shuttered, and that there would be no trace left of all the great nightspots on 133rd Street, or if someone had told me that the immortal Fats Waller had only a few more years of his young life to live, that one of the greatest young tap dancers in the country— Bill Bailey, Pearl's brother—would soon overdose and die from heroin, and that tap itself would begin to die, I would have said, "Impossible. It can't happen." Thank goodness tap was revived.

I knew such things were impossible, out of the question, incomprehensible, absurd. Whole worlds don't just collapse. Lives don't dry up, blow away to be forgotten. Certainly not a life as glorious as Harlem's. Because Harlem was young and vibrant it was going to change the world and it was going to live forever—just like me and all my friends.

I grew up all over New York. It seemed like we were moving every fifteen minutes. My father was a coachman, and he owned a couple of stables, one downtown, in lower Manhattan, and another out in Harrison, New Jersey. He made a pretty good living renting horses and boarding them for other people.

I remember my mother only vaguely. She was a beautiful woman, from her pictures. She died when I was three, and Dad never remarried.

The problem of what to do with me was quite a dilemma. I had two sisters and a brother who were much older, and I was what was known as the "unexpected" child. My parents were getting on in years when they were hit with the big surprise—me. So the responsibility of raising me fell to the younger of my sisters. If she had not volunteered to care for me, I would have gone to an orphanage. As it happened, she was the only mother I ever really knew—and a wonderful one.

None of my ancestors were in show business. I was the oddball. My brother, Walter, was the star of our family. He was a great basketball player. He could fly. Put him in a gym or on the corner tar and he soared. He was an all-American inducted into the Bob Douglas Hall of Fame and was well known throughout the city of New York. He was the star of the family, no question. We all revered him.

Early on, I wanted to be a doctor. I thought I'd like to heal the sick. Little did I know that I'd spend my life raising the dead—or with a bit of magic, making a dead, dark theatre spring back to life every night.

I started out in public school, in a little red schoolhouse on Fifty-eighth Street and Tenth Avenue. Then I moved to a school on Sixty-third Street, where there were other things besides science class that I enjoyed—namely, dancing and athletics. Basketball and track were my sports. I did okay in both in high school, but I knew I'd never be as outstanding as Walter was. Maybe in the back of my mind I had a seed of an idea of what my future held. I always loved to dance whenever someone slapped one of those thick old shellac records on the Victrola or when I heard one of the local piano greats going at it in some corner saloon. But it never occurred to me that hoofing would ever be more than a habit and a hobby for me.

The orientation of a young black kid in New York City was difficult in those days. You had to be aware of what you were doing. You had to know how to handle yourself, because there was a black-and-white struggle; there was prejudice—even back in elementary school.

I lived in a neighborhood called the Jungle. It ran from Sixty-first to Sixty-fourth streets between Tenth and Eleventh avenues, and it was all black. At Sixty-fifth Street the Irish section started. And we had a jolly fighting time with each other. We fought all the way to school, which was three blocks. Then, at twelve o'clock, we'd run home for lunch and everybody would be shoulder-to-shoulder—no problems, no hassles, no tussles at all. At one o'clock we'd come back to school for the afternoon session—and after school it would be right back to bullying each other all over again.

At three o'clock, we'd run over to Eleventh Avenue and the train tracks, where the New York Central line ran through. We'd pick up nuts and bolts and chunks of brick and mortar that were lying around and stuff them into our school bags. Our school bags were our maces, and garbage-can tops were our shields. We thought of ourselves as warriors, fighting Knights of the Round Table—the black kids versus the Irish kids. We'd swing our bags over our heads and nobody would come too close. The fights we fantasized about never really happened; nobody wanted to get into any hand-to-hand combat. We'd take our school bags full of bricks down to Eleventh Avenue, and the brick contest would start. We'd spend hours throwing bricks at each other.

Later on, when we moved uptown, the thinking was on a more progressive level. We didn't worry about throwing bricks at each other. We wanted to fight for rights, not fight just to fight and prove our might.

The most exciting school in New York was up in Harlem—P.S. 89, located at 135th Street and Lenox Avenue. This is the school that created the ungraded class. The ungraded class became a regular joke. When I started doing comedy, I could talk about the ungraded class and people would just fall out from laughing. The ungraded class was for people who couldn't be graded in any normal way—an in-between class for kids who were too dumb to go to the next grade and too old to stay where they were.

In my act, I would say, "Can I hear from the alumni of P.S. 89?" And the people in the audience would scream. I'd tell them that P.S. 89 was the greatest learning and educational school in the whole entire world—nothing surpassed it. It was the only school hardly anyone ever graduated from. You just stayed there until you were sixteen and then they gave you your walking papers. You didn't graduate— you were voted out of school. At that school people got so big, they had to bring in special chairs because nobody could fit in those little desk seats. Most of the students studied sitting and majored in sleeping. The teacher would ask them a question and they would answer with a snore and a whistle. There's no question that the school was a unique institution.

I attended high school in the Bronx. Then I did a semester at New York University. That's when I began to think that maybe doctoring wasn't for me.

If there had been an Amateur Night in Harlem in those days, I would have entered. But it was in the many small clubs around the NYU campus that I got my start as a dancer. Before I knew it, I was a college dropout. I quit school and never looked back. I thought I knew what I was doing, but really it was beyond my control. I had that overpowering desire to absorb some greasepaint and be heated by the footlights.

I was just a kid when I started going to all the clubs and hanging out with show people, trying to figure out what show business was about. Between auditions and a few small stage parts, I began to learn the business side of show business. I used to sit and listen to all the old performers who hung around an old-timers' club, in an aged brownstone up in Harlem. It was like a Friars Club, though not as elegant. The old men would sit and do much talking and bragging, and I would do a whole lot of listening. The walls of the club were plastered with pictures of the greats from past eras. There were shots of old minstrel-show players and players from the pickaninny shows that preceded minstrels. There were also pictures of Black Patti, Florence Mills, and William Cook.

The club's most famous regulars were Bert Williams and George Walker, of the comedy team Williams and Walker. Walker was a great dancer and straight man, and Williams was the comic. Williams later went solo and became a star in the Ziegfeld Follies and white vaudeville. Bert Williams (whose real name was Egbert Williams) was a star before I was born. He was the first great black crossover act, and he was ultramodern. He taught me the importance of a performer keeping his pride and dignity. Some performers would get around white people and they would start to Tom—they would act different, trying to ingratiate themselves. It was master-slave thinking. Bert Williams taught by example that that wasn't necessary. Bert wrote and recorded a series of comic monologues that were fabulous. One story has him walking down the street, slipping on a banana peel, falling down a coal chute, breaking his leg, and getting arrested. In court, he's brought before mean old Judge Grimes, who sentences him for "sliding on the sidewalk without a permit, breaking up and ruining whatever you hit; unlawful entry . . ." Bert always threw in a kernel of truth and pathos in his comedy. He understood people, and audiences related to him the way movie audiences related to Chaplin. He knew what made people tick.

In those days even Bert had to wear burnt cork. But he was not a Tom. Nor was his partner. George Walker gained fame dancing the cakewalk, a style dating back to slave days, when couples who amused the masters in the big house with the most eccentric dance steps were awarded cakes as prizes. But George Walker transformed the cakewalk into a high-style promenade. By rejecting the old, shuffling "Yazuh boss" trend, he brought class top hat and tails to the cakewalk and made it a work of art.

One of the things I learned at the old-timers' club was that the history of black show business was a history of exploitation. Many of the entertainers I talked with had been terribly jerked around.

Almost all of them were left with no money. Hell, most of them were broke. All they had left were their wonderful memories. And their fond nostalgia sounded to me like tales of tremendous hardship.

Black performers were exploited because they didn't have knowledge of the latter half of the phrase "show business." So I made it a point to learn all I could about the business. I wanted to know where the money was going to be when I came offstage. And I found that the old-timers were willing to talk about their experiences. But the number of young people who wanted to sit down and listen were few. I was different. I was interested in who they were and what they did and how they did it and what happened to their money and why their managers got rich and were living in Westchester while the performers were poor and living in cold-water tenement apartments with no electricity.

All those old performers are dead and gone now. Their world is forgotten. But what was done to them should never be forgotten. The way they were abused and misused in every manner before they died was inexcusable. I remembered the oldsters when I started Amateur Night. And to this day I make sure that the ones who are going to make a career of performing understand the business behind the great show.

When I was coming up, I was fortunate. I didn't have to struggle for years in tough living conditions like so many other performers. For most youngsters, show biz meant years on the TOBA or Chitlin Circuit through the Jim Crow South, playing segregated theatres for low pay and with little real hope for the future. Luxuries were unheard of. Compared to the long lean years so many of my contemporaries suffered through, I had it relatively easy.

Right at the beginning of my career, I got the kind of break that all young performers dream about but rarely enjoy. I was "discovered" by a gifted man who happened to be my biggest idol: the great Eddie Rector asked me to be his partner. Eddie was an established artist, one of the smoothest dancers around. He was one of the best ever, if not *the* greatest black tap dancer of his day. It was as if Michael Jackson walked into the Apollo and asked one of our amateurs to be his partner.

Also, Earl Carroll, producer of the famous *Vanities*, suggested we become a dance team because our styles complemented each other. At that time, Eddie was on top, and every young hoofer was copying

The great, the one and only, my partner, my mentor, my dear friend—Eddie Rector, one of the all-time dance geniuses. In the early 1930s Rector and Cooper played the country's leading vaudeville houses. Eddie had style, grace, and an enormous talent. I'll always love him for sharing it with me. We were truly a dream team. I wish Eddie could have stuck around to enjoy the future. You would have loved the show, old pal.

his sophisticated, fluid style. But I was not. I had my individual thing; I was doing Russian knee falls and other athletic, extremely strenuous steps, while Eddie was all grace and elegance.

Ours was what was known as a "class act," playing class theatres with a dress code that was innovative for dancers, especially black dance acts. We would come onstage in tails, in a variety of colors, top hats and spats, and we'd open the act together, dancing in tandem. Then I would come out alone and set the stage for Eddie,

Louis Armstrong, a great talent and a great friend. The first few times he played the Apollo, I couldn't figure out what that sweet aroma was that filled the theatre as soon as he started to blow.

who then did his featured solo routine. It was the epitome of tap dance—Eddie was that polished. Finally, we closed the act together, dancing in sync, shoulder to shoulder. The way we moved together, tapping in unison, perfectly in time, you could close your eyes and think one person was dancing.

We were known for our elegant style, something that was emulated by many of the team dancers, duos and even trios, that came after us, including Honi Coles and Cholly Atkins, two outstanding dancers.

Rector and Cooper toured throughout the country, playing the best venues. We were a big crossover act and played the big-time theatres, including RKO's vaudeville showcase, the Palace in Times Square. At one point, we were on the Paramount Circuit, which was white vaudeville all the way, and we opened many, many clubs and theatres, meaning we were the first black act ever to perform in many of them. I believe we were, in fact, the only black act to play the entire Paramount circuit.

Many times, Eddie and I would have to double, which meant we'd play two theatres in each town, or we'd perform at the Paramount and then double afterwards at the top club in town. Once, in Chicago, Rector and Cooper were doubling at the Sunset Cafe, which was owned by Joe Glaser. They had a house band that was just unbelievable. It wrenches the mind to think that their little old house band had Earl Hines on piano and Louis Armstrong on trumpet and a drummer named Tubby Hall who was just fantastic. Louis Armstrong used to say you could leave the club, go home and eat, take a nap, and come back and Tubby would still be on the beat. And there was no talent anywhere the equal of Louis Armstrong. He was the baddest thing since Jesse James. Guys would sit around and take notes on his solos, trying to figure out how he did the things he did with a horn. He was the master.

No matter how popular Louis became, he never forgot where he came from. He grew up in an orphanage in New Orleans, and maybe that made him appreciate what he had; it gave him a sense of humility, knowing that he could have it all one minute, and the next, fate could leave him with nothing. Louis was a motherless child. It gave him a hunger he never forgot.

Back when Louis played the Sunset Cafe and Rector and Cooper were together, Joe Glaser ran a chain of clubs for the mob. But he got respectable in later years as he became known primarily as Louis Armstrong's manager. Louis had all the faith in the world in Joe; he'd do anything Joe said. But Louis did have a mind of his own. He was probably the most famous black musician in America, if not the world. He was friends with presidents, heads of state. But he always knew who he was. And he was not a Tom—absolutely not. He proved it when he was willing to speak out at the risk of losing everything, which is what happened during the Little Rock integration crisis. Playing his trumpet, blowing the house down with his horn, that's what Louis lived for. But at the very height of his popularity, Louis Armstrong was almost put out of business.

During the civil rights struggle in the 1950s, things got very ugly down south. Segregationists didn't want to let go, and police were turning loose the dogs and arresting people who protested the injustices. Even little children were caught up in the violence. They were killed in bombings; they were harassed and kept out of schools. At the same time, the people who were throwing stones and spitting on little black kids received full protection from the police. In 1957, after Arkansas refused to let some little black kids go to school, Louis told reporters that he was ashamed for his country. He accused America of being un-American. "They would beat Jesus," Louis said, "if he was black and marched."

There was a terrific uproar. A blacklist was started against Louis, who had shows and entire tours canceled. Of course Louis could have come out and said he was misquoted and that he was sorry for what he said. But he didn't do that. Instead, he explained all over again that he felt shame for his country, watching police beat up on innocent people. Some very prominent people, white *and* black, joined the attacks on Louis. But Louis never rolled over. He lost some gigs and had some TV shows canceled; but he stood up for his people, and some of us never forgot that.

Like Chicago, Philadelphia was another swinging town in the twenties, thirties, and forties. Philly had a pair of beautiful, ornate theatres, the Fox and the Pearl. Also it had the Standard Theatre—a TOBA house. Eddie had told me so many tales about the Standard Theatre that when we played the Fox Theatre in Philly we decided that, in between shows, we'd catch the Standard Theatre show. Fortunately the time frame allowed for this; however, it was rushed. In order to do it, we had to go to the Standard dressed, ready for our next appearance at the Fox. The theatre had one of the old-time curtains that rolled up from the bottom. At the opening of the show, the curtain rolled up and there was a set with a yard in the foreground and a house in the back. Bilo and Ashes, the comics, were lyin' out in the yard. It was twilight, and the audience knew they were asleep because they could hear them snoring and whistling. Then the lights came up slowly and everyone realized that Bilo was snoring and Ashes was whistling. I rolled out of my seat. These guys were so lazy, snoring was too big a job for them—they split up the work!

Ken Bluet, who eventually became the manager of the Regal Theatre in Chicago, was working as captain of the ushers when I was appearing there. Ken's outfit was pure white—white Eton jacket and pants and a white bellboy-type hat. One morning we were rehearsing a circus show. They had a whole zoo of performing animals onstage—monkeys, horses, and a playful ape that was loose, running all over the stage, dancing around with the girls. There was also a caged lion. Ken came down the aisle to announce the theatre would open in five minutes. The ape walked over and opened up the lion's cage. The lion jumped out and made his announcement—a roar that made the MGM lion sound like a pussycat. He roared like he hadn't eaten a man in a week. Ken must have looked delicious to him, because the lion took a leap at him, right over the footlights.

Ken took off up the center aisle and ran out the door into the beautiful marble lobby with the lion, the trainer, and the ape behind him. Outside the glass doors the crowd of customers waiting to be admitted to the theatre saw the show of their lives when Ken hit that marble floor, slipping and sliding, with a giant male lion charging after him. Ken flew across the floor, hit the wall, turned, closed his eyes, and started to pray. The lion went into a crouch and pounced. Poor Ken figured it was all over. The lion slammed his paws into Ken's shoulders and pinned him up against the wall.

Ken figured the lion was going to kill him slowly and toy him to death. But the lion reared back and, instead of biting him, rolled out his huge, rough old tongue and began to lick Ken in the face. Those big, rough, wet kisses left Ken in hysterics. He started giggling and couldn't stop. By then the trainer had reached Ken and the lion, and the ape, who was jumping all over with delight, chased them both right back onstage. It was suggested that Ken be immediately dispatched to the laundromat.

There is another incident that happened at that theatre I would like to share with you. But in order to appreciate it, let me first describe the Regal to you. It was a beautiful theatre that could accommodate some 350 patrons. The theatre, with its beautiful marbled lobby and soft comfortable seats, was carpeted from front to rear. The orchestra pit was recessed and would rise as the music began. There were some thirty-five musicians under the direction of Dave

Peyton. The onstage band was electronically tracked and could be moved in four directions. The only thing I could never understand is that with all the planning and modern equipment in the Regal why the toilets were so small. Actually many people who were paying no attention to their calories had to—once in—maneuver to get out. This is the jist around which the incident was centered.

A packed theatre on a pleasant evening was engrossed in listening to the orchestra play the overture to "William Tell" and in watching the wild direction of its leader Dave Peyton whose tuxedo carried a mirrorlike shine. About midway through the overture a lady seated ten or twelve rows back from the orchestra pit calmly stepped out in the aisle, pointed a gun toward the orchestra, and commenced shooting. Indescribable confusion erupted throughout the theatre. Gunshots have that kind of magic. But the most magical feats that evening were performed by the band members who were scrambling to crawl onstage and run to safety backstage. Instruments were dropped and stepped on. Violins, bass, cellos were ruined. Two musicians toppled backward onto the drums and tore them up. But the most amazing happening was the fact that six musicians stuffed into one of the small toilets—how they did this I will never know.

About an hour after things calmed down the banging on the toilet door and the calls for help were noticed. The big problem was since the door opened in, there was no way to unhinge the door from the outside. In the meantime, the six guys inside were dying. Finally, the Fire Department who were already on the scene along with the ambulance and police used crowbars and an acetylene torch to release the door and maneuver the trapped guys to safety.

The woman who fired the shots, which might well have been blanks, disappeared in the confusion. The theatre audience, most of whom were now in the street, were sharing thoughts on their experience. The musicians were trying to pick up the pieces of their broken instruments and the guys caught up in the toilet were having their heads ventilated at the hospital. The shootout at the Regal "OK Corral" was the talk of the town, superseded only by the question, "Who was the culprit the lady was shooting at?" Needless to say, no one had any idea.

In Chicago, I met Cab Calloway. I was convinced that he had talent—long before the world heard of him and his cocaine-addicted friend, Minnie the Moocher, at New York's Cotton Club. He became the most flamboyant bandleader around. He was just outrageous onstage, a cross between Michael Jackson, Prince, and Sly Stone. With his long hair and his white coattails flying, he was a fantastic sight. I was happy to have helped and encouraged him in his career.

Cab was a great performer, no question. But offstage, Cab was something else. Around the time Joe Glaser gave Cab his shot, Cab got in an argument with another singer who was working in Chicago at the time, a red-headed character named Roscoe Simmons, from New York, whom everybody called Red. Red was playing at the Plantation, which was right across the street from the Sunset. At the Armory in Chicago at that time, they had a series of special-attraction fights for amateurs. This was an event where two city councilmen or a lawyer and a cop or any local celebrities could take their argument into the ring and duke it out for three rounds. So Cab and Roscoe got in some b.s. argument about who was the better singer or the better dancer or some such thing, and they signed up for a fight at the Armory.

Cab was a beautiful man. He was young and trim and athletic, and he looked like he could whip hell out of Red, who always looked like he had about fifteen minutes to live. Cab was taking this fight very seriously, and he asked me to help him train. So I got Cab in good shape working out on the big bag and the speed bag at the gym and road-running in the morning.

One night, I ran into Red in an after-hours joint. He was sitting at the bar, drinking down the booze, smoking and hanging out all night. I said, "Red, it's only fair I tell you, man. You better train. Cab's training every day. You got to get in shape or you're gonna get hurt."

"Aw, Coop," Red said, "you know I'm from New York, baby. I got my fight plan all laid out. The fight starts—*bong*—I'm out at the bell. I meet Cab in the center of the ring and *bam*—right in the nose. That's my plan. I just hit him right in the nose and I got him. The sucker is mine!"

"Okay, Red," I said, "have it your way. But I just want you to know, Cab's training, and he's gonna be ready for you."

Eddie and I were doubling the week of the fight, and I couldn't get to the gym every night, so I got a pro fighter I knew to train Cab. On the night of the fight, Eddie and I were running late. We had a car waiting for us, but we still couldn't make it to the Armory on time. We walked in and saw that the place was packed, but everybody inside was already going wild. People were screaming and falling all over themselves laughing and hooting. The fight was already over.

Eddie and I went to the dressing room, and there was my fighter, all dressed up in a beautiful robe. But Cab's nose was bleeding, and I realized the fight was definitely over.

I got the blow-by-blow from Cab's trainer. Cab had entered the ring looking beautiful. He had on a big white robe and satin boxing trunks and white shoes with tassles, just like Muhammad Ali used to wear. Then Red marched out like Mike Tyson—he had nothing on but a pair of trunks and sneakers. No robe. No shirt. No socks. No diamonds. Nothing. Just a towel around his neck.

The two fighters met in the middle of the ring. They shook hands. The bell sounded. Cab started dancing toward the middle of the ring— moving—bobbing and weaving—shadow-boxing, throwing jabs. Red moved out like John L. Sullivan—stiff as a dead man, his arms high and his fists out in front of him like a statue. People started to hoot Red out of the ring. But Red marched on. Cab danced out, and when they met in the middle—BOOM—Red socked him square on the nose. Cab raised his glove to feel his nose and—BOOM—Red caught him with a second shot right on the nose.

Cab was in shock. Red hit him with four or five more punches right on the end of his nose, and Cab just sat down in the middle of the ring, bleeding all over his nice whites. Cab raised his hands: *"No mas, no mas."* Then he got up off the canvas and went back to the dressing room.

That was the end of my career as a fight manager—and Cab's as a boxer. But Cab and I were friends. I kept Cab close to me because we were working the same clubs. Then one day I found out Eddie and I were being booked to cover for an act that had gotten sick on the road. And we were going to be gone about six weeks. At that time, I had a girl there in Chicago. I didn't want to just leave her, and I couldn't take her along, so I asked Cab to do me a favor. I figured he owed me, since I had helped get Joe Glaser to agree to putting him out front, which was the thing that really turned his career around. So I figured that instead of just letting my girl roam around, I would have Cab look out for her. I said to Cab: "Listen, man, I've got to go out on the road. I want you to look out for my girl—make sure everything's cool, you know? I hate leaving her alone, but you know what the business is like. So watch over her for me, will you? Make sure she gets her table at the club; take her out to dinner, keep her company—okay?''

"Sure thing, Coop," Cab said.

So I left for the tour feeling good about me and my girl. I figured with Cab looking after her, everything was copacetic. Six weeks later, I came back missing my baby bad. The first thing I did when I got off the train was find a telephone. I went right to it and called her. "Hey, baby, it's me."

"How are you?" she said.

"I'm fine. Listen, I just got in. I'm on my way from the train. Tell you what—I'll come by and pick you up. Then I'll go back to the hotel, clean up, and we'll have a nice big dinner at your favorite restaurant. What do you say?''

"Wait a minute," she said. "I'll let you talk to my husband."

"I love a girl with a sense of humor," I thought. "What a great joke!" I said, "Your *what*?"

"My husband," she said.

Then Cab got on the phone. "Hey, man," he said.

As soon as I heard Cab's voice, I knew everything was all right. "Oh, man," I said, "you guys really had me goin' there for a minute. She really had me believing it. My best friend and my best girl. You really got me, man. That's a helluva joke, pullin' my leg like that."

"Listen, Coop," Cab said. "I don't know how to tell you this, but it ain't no joke. We got married two weeks ago. I thought you'd understand. She's a helluva girl, Coop. You should never have let her go."

After that, I didn't see too much of him anymore. And I always wondered how Cab managed to convince himself that he was doing me a favor by marrying my girl. I was always careful after that when somebody asked to borrow my house for the weekend. I had to make sure they didn't do me any favors like Cab did and move in for good.

My relationship with Eddie Rector lasted a good deal longer. Eddie and I were together quite a few years, and things went well between us the entire time. I think it was because we respected each other.

Eddie was a stellar dancer. I couldn't hold a candle to Eddie. He

After Eddie and I broke up, I went back on the road with my own orchestra, the Kongo Knights. It was a hot band that could really swing and entertain. Some nights during the early years of the Apollo, I would lead the band and emcee at the same time.

was my idol. But, unfortunately, it was I who went up and Eddie who went down.

Eddie met a dancer whom he fell in love with, madly. She was booked to go to London with the Lew Leslie Blackbird Show, so she encouraged Eddie to go with her. Europe was where it was at, she told him. People were treated equally over there; Europeans were color-blind, and an artist could be judged by his art, not his color. Eddie followed his love to London, and I stayed in New York.

I had no trouble finding work. I put a swing band together. I played alto sax and I did some singing and some dancing. Ralph Cooper and his Kongo Knights toured all over the country. We even split billing at the famous Palace Theatre on Broadway with Milton Berle—and the Palace was *the* theatre in vaudeville.

The great trumpeter Roy Eldridge was in my band, as well as drummer Big Sid Catlett and saxophonist Booker Pittman. Eventually

I went to the Lafayette and then the Apollo—and the rest is the history I'm telling here. Things went well for me.

But not so well for my old partner. By the time Eddie and his wife got back to the States, just a year or two later, things had changed. Show business had turned around that quickly; nobody was interested in a man-and-woman dance team, even one starring the great Eddie Rector. Eddie fell on hard times and never really recovered. He was a genius of a dancer, and virtually illiterate, but he could count money better than any banker. When he couldn't find work, he drank. Eddie never got his career going again, but he was one of the greats! A master in the art of Terpsichore.

7

The War Years

★ ★

JOHNNY COMES BEBOPPING HOME

On December 7, 1941, I was onstage at the Apollo doing the Sunday-afternoon show. Right in the middle of my monologue a soldier in uniform walked down the middle aisle and marched straight to the foot of the stage. "Can I speak to you for a minute?" he said.

I figured this was some kind of gag—Clarence or somebody must have put this guy up to it: "Yeah, man, we'll really get Coop going." So I threw a gag back at him. "Your tank just left without you, Sarge."

But he stood his ground and said, "I would appreciate it, sir, if you would announce that every serviceman in this theatre is ordered to report to his base immediately. The Japanese attacked our naval base at Pearl Harbor in the Hawaiian Islands this morning. All active servicemen are to report to duty immediately."

I said, "This is a gag, right?"

"No, sir," he said.

Something about him—his total seriousness—made me believe him. I made the announcement, and there was an audible gasp from the crowd, then a shocked silence. A few servicemen got up to leave the theatre.

In jest, I said to the audience, "Well, we'll take care of those

Japanese in about fifteen minutes. So you guys hurry back and catch the second act.'' That lightened things up enough to go on with the show.

But things were never the same again.

While World War II ravaged the world, it raised expectations for millions of black Americans. Up in Harlem there had never been slave thinking. But in the rest of the country, especially in the South, blacks had not completely freed themselves from the slave-master syndrome. During the war, black men traveled and saw the world and were able to make comparisons with America. They learned to handle guns, and that helped them overcome their fears. Black men stood up and fought for their country, and with that came a fundamental change in attitude: ''If I can stand up for my country, I can stand up for myself and I can stand up for my people.'' After World Wars I and II, Korea, and Vietnam, black men knew how to react when the Ku Klux Klan said, ''We're gonna march through the black community.'' Before, everybody would run and hide. Now, when the KKK said the sheets were coming, they said, ''Beautiful, baby—come on down and dig our neighborhood hospitality.''

That spirit spread throughout the country. Before the war, when people were told, ''Sorry, we don't serve no Negroes in here,'' they would say, ''Okay, I'll eat somewhere else.'' But folks became more militant. They said, ''You won't serve us? That's too bad, because nobody's gonna get served in here until we do. We're not leaving— we're staying!''

Show business also felt the effects of World War II. Our most popular musical styles went through permanent change. We went swinging off to war and came bebopping home. And when that happened, the big bands broke up or shrunk to small combos. The purely practical reason was that the war caused a tremendous manpower shortage. It was tough to keep a huge orchestra together when everybody under thirty-five was drafted into service.

As the big bands began to diminish, theatres began to change. Chorus lines thinned, from sixteen high-steppers to eight to six to none at all. The small clubs became the new entertainment scene. A bandstand didn't have to accommodate a twenty-five-piece orchestra, nor was a chorus line needed. Thus the tab show and its revue became an endangered format. When there were no more big production numbers, they let the producers go, and they let the house bands out, and the staffs of costume people and set designers were all pared way down. That meant that the whole world of show business that we brought to the Apollo in 1934 was gradually fading.

Only traces of it survived. Radio City Music Hall tried to keep the tradition alive with the Rockettes. Jackie Gleason used the tab format for his television show, which lasted through the sixties. And Ed Sullivan, to some extent, used the vaudeville format: there were no chorus lines, but he would bring on comics, jugglers, and dancers who would do their thing around the featured entertainment. Today the format endures on some televised award shows. Now and then an old-style Harlem revue is resurrected on Broadway in shows such as *Black and Blue* and *Bubblin' Brown Sugar*. Johnny Carson still uses a big band, and he does his monologue and introduces variety acts. But the glorious old tab-show tradition has nearly vanished. It's as if

Erskine Hawkins toured with a smaller orchestra.

Big theatrical productions like this one, re-created for *The Duke Is Tops*, were no longer feasible at the Apollo.

a great ship had sunk and the ocean closed over it. Five minutes later, there wasn't a clue that a great ocean liner had just vanished on that very spot.

During the war years Amateur Night in Harlem continued to flourish. The high-voltage suspense and variety of budding talent kept pouring in while the world turned upside down. Some of my most cherished memories from those days were nights when my dad, Solomon, came to see the show. If there were no seats left when he came in, an usher would bring a chair down the aisle and set it up for him right in front of the stage. When I opened the show, I would tell the audience, "Folks, that's my dad there." He'd take a bow, and the audience would give him a big hand. An act would leave the stage and I'd say, "How about that, Pop?" For a stretch of about a year,

The war years were lean ones for many musicians, but Lena Horne continued to build a second career. Here she steams up the screen in *Stormy Weather*.

he'd come in every week, and when the stagehands saw him coming through the side door on 126th Street, they'd get his chair out for him. He'd be there in his nice big comfortable chair and I'd aim some of my jokes at him.

Of all the young singers who dared the Apollo audience on Amateur Night, none was more polished and sure of her talents than a skinny young church singer from Newark, New Jersey, named Sarah

Natty Nat "King" Cole was one of the great young singers who survived the demise of the big bands.

Vaughan, who came to the theatre in October 1942. Sarah was so thin and so young, I thought she had tagged along with an older brother or sister. She wore a long evening gown but still looked like the kind of girl you'd see in a small country church choir. When I heard she wanted to compete in Amateur Night, I thought about talking her out of it. She seemed so tiny, I thought the roar of the crowd would knock her off her feet. But as soon as I heard her sing, I knew she was an exceptional talent. I was so impressed by her in-depth soul and her ability to vocalize change around the melody and extend over at least five octaves. Sarah Vaughan was a superstar in the making. I wasn't the only one impressed by Sarah. Earl "Fatha" Hines, one of the all-time great eighty-eight key burners, was so amazed when he heard her, it took him three weeks to get his mouth closed.

The incomparable Sarah Vaughan won an Apollo amateur contest in 1942 at the tender age of sixteen. Here, she visits the WMCA radio studios, where I had a top-rated show.

I'd been back from Hollywood for a year, emceeing Amateur Night and working as a booking agent and independent producer at clubs around town, but Amateur Night was still the hottest ticket in town. Every show was a surprise. You never knew what was going to happen next. A truck driver with lead feet could stumble through his soft shoe and I'd have to hold Porto Rico back because the audience was being polite. The next week, the same guy could come back for his triumphant encore and get booed offstage as soon as he rolled up his sleeves to show his tattoos.

I must have heard more bad renditions of "God Bless America" than Kate Smith could stand. Today amateurs come on and sing the top radio hits of the day by Anita Baker or Michael Jackson or Whitney Houston or whoever is at the top of the pops. This can be dangerous, because the audience is so familiar with the original that a poor imitator will have the audience shouting for the guillotine after just four bars. It was the same way in the war years. It's not that people didn't like "God Bless America"—it's got a good beat and you can march to it, but listen to it every Wednesday for five years and you'd boo too.

So when Sarah Vaughan told me she had chosen to sing "Body and Soul," I had my doubts. There were two great and favorite renditions by Coleman Hawkins and Billie Holiday which everybody could hum. The audience could have hummed it in perfect harmony while booing her offstage. Sarah was going to try and win the audience over by the sheer beauty of her singing voice. I knew Sarah had the talent and the technique, but I had no idea if she could handle the pressure of the moment. Putting a sweet innocent girl with an angel's voice on that stage and asking her to woo an audience—that would boo a dear relative if she was off-key—is always a risky thing. It's like asking a soloist in the church choir to sing on a Bourbon Street corner during Mardi Gras.

But Sarah went out and did a job on that audience. When she sang she jumped octaves like she owned them. She was in key and on tone and on her way to the top. She sang with such poise and precision, if you closed your eyes you'd be sure she was about forty and had just flown in from the Paris Opera.

Sarah won the show that night, which meant she won twenty-five dollars and a week on the bill at the Apollo. And her timing couldn't have been better. My good friend Billy Eckstine happened to be in the theatre. Billy, who was the vocalist in Earl Hines's band and an Amateur Night winner himself in the late thirties, heard Sarah that night and urged Earl to hire her. Earl signed Sarah and hired her as vocalist, which was quite an honor coming from Earl Hines. Later, in June 1944, when Billy Eckstine formed his own band, he took Sarah with him as his vocalist.

Billy had a knack for bringing together musical geniuses. Maybe it started when he lived in the same apartment building with Dizzy Gillespie at 2040 Seventh Avenue, an address sometimes known as "the Musician's Building"—and for good reason. He and Diz and other young players passed their time working out new music on Diz's old upright piano. When Billy formed his big band, it had enough talent in it for ten: Dizzy, Charlie "Bird" Parker, Art Blakey, Budd Johnson, Fats Navarro, and a little trumpeter from Juilliard named Miles Davis. They were the most innovative thing going and made a lasting impact on American music by pioneering an exciting new jazz sound called bebop.

All the young musicians were caught up in the excitement of bebop. The fast, fresh staccato and the breaking of rhythmic rules fit with the new freedom the war was bringing blacks. The sound lent itself to the new small combos springing up in the wake of the demise of the big bands—that's at least part of the reason bebop spread like it did. Soon any outstanding specialist on horn could surround himself with four or five hot pieces and really do a job.

The greatest young stars of bebop were Bird and Diz, who had played in Earl's band when he played the Apollo in the forties. Charlie was a genius, no question about it. They called him the Bird because when he blew, he was in flight. He would take off. "That's the Bird, man, but with bebop, you got to be down with it to understand it, you dig?"

When the Eckstine band broke up in 1947, that pretty much spelled the end of big-band jazz. After that, big bands were the exception, not the rule. Both Diz and "Bird" went on to become deities as soloists. And Sarah Vaughan became the premier bebop vocalist. She and singers like Betty Carter and Ann Robinson were among the few who could handle bebop, because of its challenging complexities. The players improvised on the melody. That's how gifted a vocalist Sarah was. Her instrument was her voice, and she played it as well as Bird played sax and Diz played trumpet.

As bebop exploded, even "Fatha" Hines himself broke up his band and started working in small groups. Of course, he got Louis Armstrong to play in his group. Can you imagine—a small club band with Earl on piano and Pops on horn? Man, they blew down some doors!

There were a lot of people who didn't like modern jazz. Swing

Mr. Intensity, Miles Davis, blew his horn with Bird, Diz, and the rest of the big daddies of bebop. In the fifties and sixties, he helped popularize the esoteric sound. Today, Miles still turns his back on an audience now and then, just as he used to at the Apollo. Miles has always been good at blowing minds, too.

One of the great vocalists to emerge with the new sound, Betty "Bebop" Carter was an Apollo audience favorite.

157

was it. Nothing else ever interested them again once swing died out. But for me, I liked bebop. I liked R&B, and I liked soul, funk, and rock 'n roll. It's all music, and I move as it moves.

Even at the Savoy Ballroom, where big-band jazz was god, I talked Charlie Buchanan, the manager, into using a small combo. Up to that point the smallest band to ever play there had been Al Cooper and his Savoy Sultans. Al's was a band that jumped like absolute crazy—eight pieces that challenged the greatest.

But I convinced Charlie to book a little band headed by Illinois Jacquet. Illinois, who is still working today, is a great, great tenor sax player who first made his mark with the Lionel Hampton band and then played with Count Basie in 1945 and '46. Illinois came in to the Savoy with his combo and he tore the place up. He wrecked 'em. They played hard music: hard sax; big, strong beat. And they just kicked 'em all over the place. That became the vogue in Harlem and the rest of the country—small, ass-kicking combos. In other cities it was known as "New York jazz," though in fact it was Harlem jazz.

One of the cultural contributions bebop brought was beatnik jive talk. Jive is another product of Harlem, like music and dance. The latest lingo came from Harlem, just like the latest tunes and steps. It didn't start with the boppers, of course. A phrase like "Nothin' goin' on but the rent" was 1930s jive. ("What's goin' on, man?" "Nothin' but the rent.") Years later, that line became the title of a hit song. Phrases that began in Harlem soon spread through the land. In the sixties, it was "What's happenin', baby?" and "Oh, man, that's out of sight." "Gimme five" goes back all the way to the 1930s. In the forties, the beboppers changed it to "Skin me, baby." "It's bad" meant it was good. A small-timer who fancied himself a big spender was a "big butter-and-eggs man" a long time ago. Louis Armstrong called everybody "Pops" and "Cats."

But it was the beboppers who invented the hip jive. And nobody was more hip to the jive than Diz. The dark shades, the French beret cocked at a cool angle, and the goatee under the lip—Diz started that look. When he blew a wailing solo, the kids all went, "Yeah, daddy-o!"

When I was doing radio shows in the forties, Diz was the toughest—and funniest—interview I ever had. I'd spin the platters and then have the artist come on live to talk about the record we just played. Diz liked to fool around with the format. He'd tease the listeners and he'd tease me. He made fun of the fact that people couldn't see us. I'd say, "How many guys you got in the band, Diz?" He'd hold up five fingers. "Did you have a good crowd?" He'd shake his head and grin like the Cheshire cat. "How many people were there, man?" He'd spread his arms and smile like Buddha.

Unfortunately, drugs were credited with a big part of the bebop scene—especially heroin and opium. We've all heard the sad tales of "Bird" and Billie Holiday and what getting hooked on horse did for them. But at the same time, many young hipsters were naive about how some players soared so high. Dizzy had a vocalist named Joe Carroll who was a great scat man. He was one of those really high-geared speed riffers who was down with the jive but innocent to the drug scene around him. One day Joe was standing in front of a Harlem hotel. The hotel was owned by an Italian combine and it was where all the well-known performers stayed when they were in town. Joe was out front one morning, shuckin' and jivin', rappin' and laughin' and playing the hepcat role. "Heeyy, bay-bee, what's hap'nin'?"

Joe was jivin' away when around the corner came a guy who put on the same look and the same lingo. "Hey, Joe, what's hap'nin', baby?" he said.

"Everything's cool, man," Joe said. "You swingin'?"

"You know it, Joe," the guy said. "Hey, man, I'm like goin' inside the hotel, you dig? How about holdin' on to this bag for a minute, my man?"

"Okay, baby," Joe said. He didn't know the cat, but he trusted the dude's cool attitude. "Whatever makes you happy, baby."

So Joe took the bag and went right back to running off at the mouth and playing the role when around the corner came three fellas. One said, "Is that your bag?"

Joe laughed and said, "No, man, I'm holdin' it for a cat in the hotel. He'll be right out."

Faster than Joe could say "You dig?" the three squares flashed their badges and grabbed the bag. Joe, in shock, said, "Hey, baby, what's this scene, man?" The cops just cuffed Joe and took him down to the lockup. Joe tried to explain to the police. "I was just standing there and this dude whips around the corner and leaves me like holding this bag, man."

"Sure, fella," the cop said. Of course the bag was full of dope, high-grade stuff, and the police naturally didn't believe for one minute that this jive-talking hipster was innocent.

In those days you had to have a police ID card to work in a nightclub. The first thing the police did was take Joe's card, so he couldn't work. Nothing Joe could do or say could get him his card back.

I finally took him to see Percy Sutton, a young attorney with a Clarence Darrow brain. Percy had to do one helluva job to get Joe out of that mess and get him his cabaret card back. It took a while, but Percy did it.

As the big bands broke up, smaller nightclubs began to thrive. One of the most successful in Harlem was the Elks' Rendezvous, on 133rd Street at Lenox Avenue. This club held only a hundred and fifty people. Yet the owner, Johnny Barone, hired top performers and paid top dollar. They had little bitty tables—just twenty-eight inches across—and they would seat up to six people around each one. Everybody was huddled up and cozy. The place stayed packed three shows a night, and four on weekends.

In those days I was producing at the Elks' in addition to producing the Wednesday-night amateur show at the Apollo and hosting a radio show on WINS.

In the midst of all this modern attitude, I had a club encounter of the old-fashioned kind. A mounted cop was stationed outside the Elks', and I struck up a great friendship with his horse. Every night, I'd bring him carrots, a few lumps of sugar, and a bottle of beer. I knew from my dad's stable that horses love beer for the malt. I would pull down this guy's lip and pour in the beer. Then he'd stick his tongue out and try to be affectionate. One night I was late, running in to get the show started, and I ran right past the horse. I got a few steps inside when I heard this commotion behind me. I turned around and there was the mounted cop pulling the horse out of the small doorway leading into the club. The horse had bolted and come charging after me. He was thirsty, man—he wanted his beer and he wanted it now!

Some people say that bebop developed because musicians were tired of playing for dancers. That's because bebop isn't music you dance to. Others say bebop was invented by black musicians who

The Queen of the Blues, Dinah Washington was named Ruth Jones before she was discovered in Chicago, working as a ladies' room attendant. Dinah would have been a star in any era.

didn't want to play with white musicians. There were always white guys coming around for after-hours jam sessions, and the beboppers tried to cut them out by getting more and more esoteric.

I don't buy either of those explanations.

The bebop musician was a dedicated technician. He had to play around the melody and run through the chords. The main thing was technique. All the great beboppers, from "Bird" and Diz to Miles Davis, were virtuoso performers in their own right. There is no great prejudice among artists. Musicians respect one another for their ability, not their color, their clothes, or who they're dating. You are either a good musician, a fair musician, or a poor musician. You don't say,

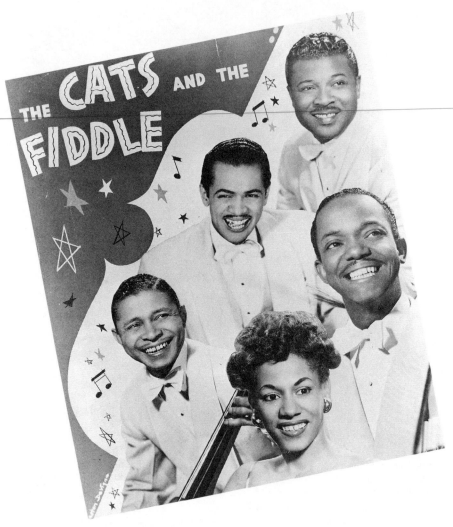

The Cats and the Fiddle was a good-time act influenced by the great Louis Jordan.

"Yeah, man, he's a great black trombonist" or "He's a great black drummer." Now, it's true, if you heard records and assumed from the way the band was swinging that it was a black band and then saw Gene Krupa on drums, you might say, "Wow, that drummer's a white fella." But it wasn't the main thing on your mind. When you see a jazz band, you don't see white and black; it's an intermingling of cultures and ethnic styles.

The Apollo was never a blacks-only showplace. We had a string of white musicians and performers onstage throughout the history of the theatre. Buddy Holly was not the first white act to play the Apollo, as they said in the movie *The Buddy Holly Story.* Charlie Barnet, the rich boy who dashed his parents' hopes of his becoming a corporate lawyer by heading up his own band on an ocean liner at age sixteen, may have been the first white star to headline. But there was no gasp or stunned silence or anything like that. It was a band, and as long as it could swing, it didn't matter what color it was. Some nights we had as many white performers as blacks—Benny Goodman, the Dorseys, Krupa, Buddy Rich, Artie Shaw. There were a number of white acts that played the Apollo before Buddy Holly.

Bebop was one branch that broke off the jazz tree in the years during and after the War. Another was a new kind of swing, the way Louis Jordan played it. Louis played jazz in a fast, funny uptempo

Another Jordan-influenced act, the Fabulous McClevertys, do some clowning.

style. And it was a style that had more in common with what was to come—rhythm and blues and rock and roll—than with bebop. A lot of the early rockers watched Louis Jordan and the way his band used to roll. He had the backbeat that would later be the driving force of rock. But Louis made a name with madcap novelty songs like "Is You Is or Is You Ain't My Baby" that showed his sense of humor. Who could resist the squawkin', rockin' classic "Caledonia," which asked the question "What makes your big head so hard?"

I first met Louis Jordan when I was appearing in Philadelphia. Louis was working in a club called the Showboat, where he was a young saxophone player leading the house band. I told him he should get out of Philadelphia and come to New York, where the action was hot. He wasn't getting anywhere by staying in Philadelphia, and he knew it. "My bags are packed," Louis said. I brought him to New York and put him in the Apollo band. Later he got a gig at the Elks' Rendezvous. Needless to say, he was a tremendous sensation.

Louis and his Tympany Five were regulars at the Elks' Rendezvous and the Apollo in the war years. He became the hottest thing going.

Louis Jordan made some of the first music videos. They were called Soundies. All the popular new bands—Nat King Cole, Artie Shaw, Benny Goodman, Gene Krupa, even older stars like Duke Ellington—made Soundies forty years before MTV.

The bands set up on sound stages and played while a camera crew filmed them. The record companies then took these high-quality short films and had dozens of prints made into film loops. Those were sent to clubs and bars that had Soundie machines—jukeboxes with a film screen attached on top. Pop in a quarter and you could see Louis Jordan and the Tympany Five doing "You're Much Too Fat" or "Five Guys Named Joe" while you sipped a highball. Soundies were of superior quality, with synchronized sound. If you can find one today you've got a real collectors' item on your hands.

Unfortunately, Soundies never really caught on. People would go to a juke joint and play the Soundie of Louis Jordan's band doing "Run Joe Run," but the rest of the night they'd want to do some dancing, so they'd play the music only, which cost just a nickel. Nobody wanted to sit there and watch the film more than once. They wanted to hear the music. There were a lot more nickels than quarters in the coin box the next morning.

Some of the magnificent ladies who graced our stage.

Among the greats who used the Apollo stage as a launching pad to the stars: (*clockwise from top left*) Bill Kenney, Johnny Mathis, Arthur Prysock, Timmy Rogers, Jimmy Rushing, Billy Daniels, Screamin' Jay Hawkins, and Billy Eckstine (*center*).

Another vocal musical style that emerged was the forerunner of doo-wop. It was made popular by the Mills Brothers, Bill Kenny, the Ink Spots, the Platters, the Cadillacs, the Orioles, and others. Bill Kenny, I'm proud to say, was another Amateur Night winner destined for greatness. He came up from Baltimore, and Moe Gale, the theatrical manager and Savoy Ballroom owner, hired him to sing with the Ink Spots. Soon Bill was the highest-paid person in the group at $900 a week. But Moe, generous soul that he thought he was, used to sell the Ink Spots for $5,000 a night against percentages.

It wasn't long before the Spots were out of the Apollo's price range, and the only time we could snare a date was when they would double at the Apollo while playing a big theatre downtown. I have often thought this unusual arrangement was designed to keep the Harlem audience uptown. Once, the Ink Spots were playing the Paramount downtown and the Apollo the same week. They'd take a limo downtown after the first show at the Apollo. But at night, the traffic got all jammed up, and they were arriving late for the evening shows at the Apollo. So Moe Gale hit on the idea of putting the group in an ambulance and running them uptown in that. Every day an ambulance zoomed them uptown to the Apollo, siren blasting, speeding through traffic. What a stunt! It not only got the group there on time, but it created a spectacle. The Ink Spots' ambulance became one of the greatest promotions we ever had, even though it was all by accident, so to speak.

Harlem was always a step ahead of the times. But during the war I saw the less progressive side of America when I organized for the army a show called the "Blue Ribbon Salute." My orders were not to play to segregated audiences throughout the camps. This was a tour to play military bases around the country. It was a fantastic group: we had Earl Hines and his band that included such revered exponents of jazz as Dizzy Gillespie, Charlie Parker, Bennie Green, Baggy Britches, Shadow Wilson, and a list that read like a who's who of jazz. We also had Louis Jordan and his Tympany Five, Sarah Vaughan, Billy Eckstine, Bill Bailey, the dance team of Patterson and Jackson, and the Four Blue Bonnets. We went all through the South and performed in military bases and towns where they'd never heard musicians like these before. Everywhere we went, we caused a sensation.

Earl Hines was a big eater. We went to a restaurant in Georgia one morning and there was a lot of excitement among the waitresses and customers because they were face to face with the biggest names in modern music. The phones started ringing and people were shouting, "Come on down, they're here!" None of this fazed Earl, who figured first things first. And food, for Earl, was always first. He said to a waitress, "What do you have for breakfast, dear?"

"Well," she said, "we have fried chicken, smothered pork chops, barbeque ribs, grits, and yams."

"Fine," said Earl. "Bring me that." The waitress was somewhat confused.

"Mr. Hines, I don't understand," she said. "Which do you want?"

"Bring me all of it—the chicken, the pork chop, the ribs, the yams, and the grits." And Earl sat there and ate all of it, then ordered a dozen chicken sandwiches to carry on the train.

Earl repeated this almost every day, and he was about as big as a matchstick. In all the years I knew him, I never saw Earl with a bit of flab on him. He never exercised except onstage and in bed, and he never dieted, yet he never got big. Count Basie, who was big, couldn't keep up with Earl when it came to eatin'. Back in New York, there was a Horn & Hardart on Broadway where they offered all you could eat for two dollars. They asked Earl not to come in there anymore.

There was some great music made on that tour. I remember one show when Charlie Parker fell asleep on the bandstand right in the middle of a number. When the chorus was over, Dizzy hit Charlie—bopped him on the head—and said, "Come on, man, it's your solo." Charlie jumped up like he'd been shot and went right into a solo—nobody but him playing. And nobody but us knew he'd fallen asleep. The audience thought that was just Charlie's way, waiting to go on with his eyes closed. They figured he was meditating on the sounds. But Charlie was nodded out. He was gone to the world, out stone-cold. Charlie was on heroin, which messed up a lot of musicians.

Another one who got all strung out was Big Maybelle. She was a wonderful singer and a funny character who did a lot of sniffin'. Heroin was her thing; and it cost a lot of money. She used to hang out at the theatre, and whenever she needed the powder, which was all the time, she would put the touch on anybody who was around. Maybelle would see Joe Louis and she'd walk up to him and start whining and crying, and Joe, whose generosity was unbelievable, would say, "What's the matter, Maybelle?"

"Oh, Joe," she'd say, "my grandmother just died, and she's gotta be buried, and I ain't got no money to go down there and take care of the funeral arrangements and all."

"Well, whatcha need, Maybelle?"

"Oh, Joe, I need train fare to get down south and attend my poor grandmother's funeral."

And Joe would peel off two hundred or three hundred dollars and hand it to her and say, "Is this enough, Maybelle?"

Maybelle would take the money, and a week later, she'd find Joe and tell him the same sob story about her poor grandma and he'd listen and sympathize and hand over the money again. One day, Joe was counting up the number of times Maybelle's grandmother had died, and he figured it was about twelve times. So Joe knew the score. He wasn't anybody's dummy. He knew she was jiving. He had the money, so he gave it to her. He was that kind of person.

I had a long friendship with Joe. The very first time he came to New York from Detroit, he visited the Apollo and I introduced him as the next heavyweight champion. This was when he was a contender. Joe was a wonderful person, fine-looking and big and gentle. He was one of the few boxers I know who would shake hands with people—most won't. He was very warm, and generous to a fault. He liked people, and sometimes they took advantage of that. He went through money something fierce. I was fortunate because of my friendship with the Champ to arrange a thirty-day one-nighter tour throughout the South, booked by the Gale Agency. Joe's management was opposed to the tour and only agreed to it when Joe said I would go with him. So I was elected to babysit the most exciting individual in the world. The show consisted of Luis Russell and his great band featuring the sensational and sensuous Betti Mays. The Champ was a bigger celebrity than any movie star, and he sold out every venue he appeared in. Joe created excitement wherever he went. Whenever he had a fight, Harlem would go wild. Everybody would listen on the radio, and when the fight was over, they poured out into the streets, banging on tin cans, everybody screaming and hollering. I felt people must feel strongly for Joe all over the country. And I knew Joe enjoyed getting out and meeting people and being the star of the show without having to get in a ring and fight. All he had to do was stand up and talk. Joe and I would do comedy crossfire, with Joe as the straight man. Then Joe would do question-and-answer sessions with the audience. They loved it. It was great fun, and Joe broke percentages everywhere we played.

For each date, $5,000 was guaranteed for Joe and $5,000 went to the promoter. That was $10,000. Whenever the take exceeded that, 60 percent of the difference went to Joe and 40 percent to the promoter. Half of Joe's $5,000 was paid at the contract signing. The other $2,500 was paid out the night of the affair, before Joe went on; and at the end of the night, whatever the split was, Joe received his cut. Joe's money was to be sent to New York, and he would get a statement every night so he knew exactly how much money he was getting. It was a fair deal, and I explained all the details to Joe. I told him that out of that nightly $2,500, he could pocket whatever he wanted. The rest would go into the bank, and he could pick it up at the end of the tour.

So Joe said, stuttering, "I-I-I-I think maybe I'll take three hundred a night."

I said, "Fine—three hundred."

When we were on our way to the first date, Joe said, "You know, Coop, I think you better make that five hundred."

I said, "Fine, Joe—whatever you say."

By the time we got to the first date he wanted a thousand. By the time the first date ended, he said, "Let me have fifteen hundred."

I said, "What do you need all of that money for?"

"I'll have it in case I need it," he said.

Later, the reason surfaced. Joe had two chicks flying in every night and two chicks flying out—every single night we were on tour.

At the conclusion of the tour, I made arrangements for Joe to meet me at the Gale Agency in New York and pick up the balance of the monies owed him. He received a check for thousands of dollars, and the first thing he said was "Where can I cash this, Coop?"

Tim Gale and a few others from the office escorted the Champ to an Irving Trust branch a few doors east of the Gale Agency at 48 W. 48th Street. As soon as we walked in, everybody crowded around, wanting to see the Champ.

Joe told the bank manager he wanted to cash his check. "You don't want me to cash the whole check, do you, Mr. Louis?" the man asked. "It's an enormous amount."

I said, "Joe, you can't walk around with this kind of money." But all I could do was get him to take half in cash and half as a bank check.

A week later, Joe's manager, a tiny, lovable guy named Marshall Myles, called me up and said, "Listen, Coop, when can we pick up the money?"

I said, "What money?"

"You know—the money from the tour."

I said, "Joe's got the money—minus the fifteen hundred he drew out every night."

Marshall said, "Do you know I was giving that bum eight hundred dollars a night on the road? That was on top of the fifteen hundred he was getting from you."

Marshall asked me to meet him at the Theresa Hotel. We went upstairs and Joe was stretched out across the bed in his shorts. Marshall went crazy. He said, "I'm mad as a bullfrog and I'm gonna beat your ass, Joe!" Now, Marshall was the size of a gnat compared to Joe. But he was mad as hell, and he jumped on Joe and started flailing away, and Joe got to laughing so hard he couldn't control himself. He was giggling hysterically, as if Marshall was tickling him.

During the tour with Joe, we went through Alabama, which is where he was from. Joe said he wanted to go see his aunt. So some of us drove off with Joe and we got to a stretch of road where we couldn't drive because it was nothing but mud—it was impassable. We were standing there in our gabardines when a farmer came along with a mule and a wagon. We stopped him and told him where we wanted to go. He said, "Sure, I know where that's at. Y'all get on in there. I'll take ya right on down."

So Joe Louis, his entire entourage, and I all climbed in behind this mule, and when we got to where we were going, the man started hollering.

"Annie! C'mere, Annie! I got somebody for you to see."

Out came Annie, and she had an apron on and a corncob pipe in her mouth. She took that pipe out, spit a block, studied Joe's face, and said, "Is that you, boy?"

Joe said, "Yes, ma'am."

She said, "Get on down off that wagon."

Man, we had a time! Word got out that Joe Louis, the Champ himself, was visitin', and people came from all around those backwoods to see him. Wagons and mules of every size and shape pulled up out front. It was Joe's first homecoming since he'd become Champ.

Backstage at the Apollo, all the musicians and performers loved to pass the time talking jive and trading stories about life on the circuits. The most amazing, preposterous stories were those told about bands traveling in the chitlin' towns of the Deep South. Crazy things happened to people down there in Dixie.

Don Redman was a great musician you don't hear much about these days—a terrific sax player and a wonderful arranger as well. He took Gershwin's *Rhapsody in Blue* and made a dance version of it. Gershwin heard about it, so he and Paul Whiteman went up to the Roseland Ballroom, where Don was playing with the Fletcher Henderson Band, to have a listen. Gershwin used to tell people that Don was "a real genius."

People tended to feel strongly about Don Redman. Once when he was on tour in the South he had a bus with a big "Don Redman Band" logo painted on the side. As the band was cruising along on the highway somewhere in the Carolinas, a car sped past the bus and then slowed way down, cutting it off. The driver waved the bus over to the side of the road. So the bus came to a stop on the shoulder, and this giant cracker got out of the car and marched back to the bus like he was the law. Then he boarded the bus like he owned the whole state of South Carolina and said, "Which one of y'all is Don Redman?"

Nobody said a word; nobody knew what to say. So Don, who was a short little guy, stood up and said, "I'm Don Redman."

The cracker looked him over and said, "By God, you're the greatest musician I ever heard. You don't need to ride with these niggers. Get on up. Come on with me. We gonna take you into town."

What could Don do? He had to go. So Don rode into town with the cracker and was stuck with him for the rest of the engagement.

There was something about Jim Crow that made people crazy. When I had the Champ down south during the tour, we stopped in a small town to buy some records and a crowd gathered around to see the great Joe Louis. People were standing there paying respect when someone began pushing from the back of the crowd. It was a little old lady. "Open up. Let me by. What's going on here?" she said.

Somebody said, "Joe Louis, the heavyweight champ, is in the record store."

"Oh, hell," the lady said, "I thought they were hangin' a nigger." Sweet old lady. She looked like Jed Clampett's momma.

Black artists ran into crazy prejudices all the time, everywhere they went. But the South was the strangest. The South was a weird place, man.

Pigmeat and I were driving through the Deep South on a promotional tour for the black motion-picture industry. We were in a beautiful, Chinese-red Packard, and whenever we'd pull into a little gas station to fuel up, some old redneck would come out and stare at us and say, "There's the water, boy. There's the gas. You know what to do."

After this happened a few times, Pig said, "Coop, next stop, let me talk to these people." So we pulled into a station and Pig got out of the car and pointed to the front end, where there was a license-plate frame with the word HOLLYWOOD in big letters.

"Hello, boss," Pig said, "I want you to be very careful with Mr. Gable's car. We're drivin' his car from Hollywood to New York for him, and we don't want anything to happen to it."

So the redneck calls inside to his wife. "Bessie," he says, "come on out here now. This here's Clark Gable's Packard." Oh, you should have seen them polish that car down!

When we got to Laurel, Mississippi, we noticed there were all these great-looking white girls in the front rows of a black theatre. So when Pig was talking to the manager, he said, "I always thought that in a black theatre, whites sat in the back, and in a white theatre, blacks sat in the back."

"That's true," the manager said.

So Pig said, "I saw all those white people in the front here and I know this is a black theatre."

"What do you mean, 'white people'?" the manager said. "There ain't no white people here today."

"I saw all those redheads and blondes, all those white women sitting down there in front."

"Oh," the manager said. And he got a big laugh out of this. "They're not white. They're second family people."

"Second family people?"

My boy and my pride and joy, Ralph II, was in the good hands of a true heroine. He is in the front row at the Apollo being held by Marian Anderson, the great contralto who became one of the guiding lights in the struggle for equal rights and human dignity after her famous concert on the steps of the Lincoln Memorial.

"Father's white, mother's black." The first rows of this segregated theatre were reserved for fair-skinned people, who were treated like they're white by the blacks!

Just before we came to this town, there was some trouble because a black man insulted one of the beautiful second family girls. She told her father about it, who was white, and he came down with four or five other crackers, found this guy in the street, and beat the hell out of him. He told the man, "If I ever hear of you talking to my daughter, I'll come back and kill you." This bully had a white family on one side of the tracks and a black family on the other. And in Mississippi, where Jim Crow was boss, it was completely acceptable, both legally and socially. Things obviously hadn't changed all that much since slavery days, when the white master would go down to the slave quarters and pick out a pretty girl and she'd end up having a baby.

I went to a party in Mississippi where there was a house full of nice-looking black teenagers. A white man came up to me and said, "My daughter's been telling me a lot about those pictures you're in. I'm gonna have to go down there and see one of them."

I said, "Well, I'd be happy to have you see one."

He said, "She's been talking about you and wanted to have a party for you. That's why we're all gathered here. This reception's for you. I got to go now, but I wanted to see you and tell you that."

And off he went. Now this was a real, shotgun-carryin' good ol' boy, and it took me a while to realize that he was the father of the young black girl who was hosting the party for me.

One of the great stories told backstage at the Apollo was about the time Claude Hopkins and his band were playing down in Charlotte, North Carolina. It got to be two o'clock in the morning and the dance was about over and Claude started playing his customary closing number, "Home Sweet Home." He was a couple of bars into it when this huge redneck climbed onstage with a gun hanging from his belt and said, "Just a minute here. I've been standing back there for nigh on an hour and I ain't heard you boys play 'Tiger Rag.' By God, you boys gonna play 'Tiger Rag' or I'm gonna take my pistol and there's gonna be some shootin' in here." Man, the trombone player didn't wait a second. "Hold that ti-ger!" For the next half-hour Claude's band played a bang-up, flag-waving version of "Tiger Rag."

Of course, artists didn't find this treatment all that amusing. Constantly running up against perverse attitudes and ignorance could give us our own warped view of things. But then an act of such kindness, generosity, or warmth would make it clear that it's not a question of black or white. We might get mistreated in Mississippi one night, but the next day we'd be in Chicago, where things were more progressive.

One of the reasons Chicago and New York were more progressive was music. I really believe that. The music helped open things up in this country. Music is a great source of understanding. You hear a record and you want to learn more about who made it. You become interested in someone else's culture and you try to understand it. I believe that Louis Armstrong, Count Basie, Fats Waller, Duke Ellington, Ella Fitzgerald, Sarah and "Bird" and Diz, Sam Cooke, James Brown, Aretha Franklin, Otis Redding, and all the rest had as much to do with advancing the cause of civil rights and equal rights in this country as the marches and demonstrations of the fifties and sixties. Listeners loved their art; and when a person opens himself to art, he opens himself to an understanding of the artists who make it. When white kids heard Louis Armstrong or any of the other great black performers, they heard that genius, and that was the beginning of the end of segregation in this country.

Rock and Roll

★ ★

SPOTLIGHT ON HARLEM

The girls who screamed for Frankie and Elvis and the Beatles weren't the first screamers in show business. As long as dudes have been moving and shaking, girls have been screaming for more. They squeal for great dancers and they rhapsodize for great singers, and the only cats who can get more of a rise are those who can dance *and* sing.

This has been true since the beginning of time. Eve was a goner the second Adam walked out onstage at the Eden, bit into that apple, and did his bump-and-grind routine. Eve lost it right then and there. She started screaming, and girls have been screaming ever since.

In the fifties, screaming was the main show-business sound. It was the sound of cash registering. If the gals weren't screaming, man, you weren't happening. It started when rhythm-and-blues players became rock and rollers. The beat got the crowd rocking, and the singer got the girls rolling.

Singers became idols. They were like gods in silk suits with razor-sharp creases. And when they grabbed a mike, cocked their hips, and swaggered to the backbeat, screaming was the sound of uncontrolled excitement. With all that sexuality letting loose, things got downright hysterical. The singers knew all the secrets. And in

I broke a great many rhythm and blues and early rock artists from my live broadcast booth at the Palm Cafe, a popular nightclub on 125th Street. Here, one of the greatest gospel and rock singers of all time, Sam Cooke, drops by to chat and sing a number.

One of the founding fathers of rock and roll, piano man Antoine "Fats" Domino never got all the credit he deserves.

those days there was only one secret, which was rock and roll. That was what it was all about. It wasn't for love or money, they were singing for personal ego.

The girls who gathered outside the Apollo stage door on 126th Street in the early fifties were the first rock-and-roll groupies. They would wait for hours for autographs or a glimpse of their heartthrobs. They'd send notes and snapshots of themselves upstairs to the dressing rooms. Some would clip pictures out of magazines and send them up to Jackie Wilson or Sam Cooke, claiming they were the girls in the pictures.

The singers loved every minute of it (especially the screaming), from the first rock-and-roll idols—Johnny Ray, Johnny Ace, and Clyde McPhatter—to Bo Diddley, Hank Ballard, Fats Domino, and, later, Little Richard, Chuck Berry, and James Brown. Oh, man—James Brown, Jackie Wilson, and Sam Cooke were the top scream-getters. They had troops of girls screaming themselves hysterical.

All the singers and their managers knew it was important to keep their female fans happy. If you had the girls on your side, you were there. The women made you. They made you because they were the ones who were vociferous. The fact is, the same is true today. The guys in the audience were a little reluctant. They would be watching the singer and the girls screaming and think: "Look at that clown prancin' around up there. What's he got I ain't got? Nothin' but tight pants and a ten-dollar process." Some cats saw James Brown and all the girls swooning and decided they'd get themselves a beat and a step and a sharp suit, slick their hair back, and get out onstage and do it. That is the rock-and-roll dream. If a shoeshine boy and ex-con from Macon, Georgia, like James Brown can do it—baby, I can do it too!

Rock and roll brought a new sense of freedom that hit the performers with a jolt and jumped offstage and electrified the audience. The sexual awakening built into the panty and bra-throwing syndrome on to the stage. And it kicked off a counterculture where teens began to see nice, conservative America for what it was—racist. When kids disobeyed laws that required whites and blacks to sit on different sides of the Peacock Club in Atlanta, segregation was on the wane. All of a sudden, blacks and whites together were clapping their hands and saying, "Come on, baby, let's boogaloo."

★   ★   ★

Hey, Bo Diddley! Another early contender for the title of King of Rock and Roll. When Bo played the Apollo in the fifties, there was no doubt who had the greatest rock and roll band in the world. Buddy Holly, the Rolling Stones, George Thorogood, and countless other rock legends owe a debt to the inventor of the Bo Diddley Beat. Anyone who says different don't know Diddley.

The Apollo Theatre had as much to do with the birth of rock and roll as Sam Phillips's Sun Studio in Memphis, where Elvis Presley first recorded rhythm and blues. Before R&B crossed over, turned white, and was renamed rock and roll, there were lines running down 125th Street and around the corner onto Seventh Avenue to the east

Jackie Wilson drove the girls in the balcony—and everyone else in the theatre—wild with his knee drops and sexy moves. One of his first hits, "Lonely Teardrops," was written by a Detroit songwriter who was trying to start his own record label—Motown's Berry Gordy.

and onto Eighth Avenue to the west. On a night when Jackie Wilson or one of the other great R&B chart toppers was crooning his magic, the top balcony was always filled with screaming foxes and cool cats.

Elvis himself visited the Apollo in 1955 during his first trip to New York to appear on the Dorsey Brothers' TV show. Bo Diddley was playing that night, and that's how Elvis got his pelvis—he saw Bo make moves Elvis never saw in his mama's church down there in Tupelo.

Before Clyde McPhatter first got famous as lead singer for the Dominoes, he went against his religious parents' wishes to compete in Amateur Night. Clyde's great contribution was that he introduced black gospel to rock and roll. He took the sobbing and shouting of church music and combined it with secular rhythms. Later that sound became known as soul music. After winning Amateur Night, Clyde was signed by talent manager Billy Ward to be the lead singer of the

When Clyde McPhatter, who was seventeen when he won our Apollo Amateur Night contest around 1950, left the Dominoes Quartette, he was replaced by Jackie Wilson. Clyde went on to join the Drifters.

After Clyde left the Drifters to enter the Army in the mid-fifties, he was replaced by Benjamin Nelson, also known as Ben E. King. After Ben E. left, the Drifters scored two of their biggest hits, "Up on the Roof" and "Under the Boardwalk." Jackie, Clyde, and Ben were all Amateur Night winners.

Ben E. hit big after the Drifters, enjoying a solo hit with his classic ballad "Stand By Me."

Dominoes. He was just seventeen. Clyde's singing was sensual and passionate; songs like "Have Mercy, Baby" became huge hits and seemed to devastate the ladies. But Ward billed the band as "Billy Ward and His Dominoes." Clyde had too much pride to stomach that, so he split and joined a new group, the Drifters. His replacement in the Dominoes was another young, proud, and amazing Amateur Night winner, Jackie Wilson. Clyde was drafted into the army in 1954 and never regained his popularity. Several years later, the new Drifters scored yet another dynamic lead singer from the Amateur Night winners' circle: Ben E. King. King's real name was Benjamin Nelson, and he came on with his group the Five Crowns, one of the first Harlem vocal groups, and stopped the show with his beautiful tenor. He became a Drifter after one of the original group's members got drunk and started berating Frank Schiffman. I thought he made some good points, but the Drifters were disbanded shortly after that, and Ben's Five Crowns became the new Drifters. For my money, they were better than the originals.

A vocal group I brought up from Baltimore to play the Apollo—Sonny Til and the Orioles—helped start the doo-wop craze. I was in

Baltimore with a tour I had packaged that was playing the Royal Theatre, which was part of the Around the World circuit, along with the Lafayette in New York, the Lincoln in Philadelphia, and the Howard in Washington. I was walking around one night and this group caught me right there in the street. They said they were a quartet and all they wanted was a chance to get started. They knew who I was and they wanted a spot in my Amateur Night show at the Apollo. I said, "Well, can you sing?" They put on a show right on the spot. As soon as I heard them, I knew they'd win a week at the Apollo if they could handle the Amateur Night audience.

They handled it, all right. Sonny Til was the lead singer, and he would get down on his knees and cry and beg the girls for their lovin'. And love him they did. As soon as the Orioles finished, the audience started hollering: "Give 'em a week, Coop! Hell, give 'em *two* weeks!"

The Orioles, who were a rougher and freer updated version of the Ink Spots, were the first of the great rockin' harmony acts. Their vocal style and even their name were copied by the flock of bird groups that came after them—the Ravens, the Robins, the Skylarks, the Flamingos, the Penguins, and all the rest, including the Crows, who were another Amateur Night discovery. The Orioles influenced everybody from Smokey Robinson and the Miracles to the Temptations and Gladys Knight and the Pips. Even the Supremes, the Ronettes, and all the girl groups used the Orioles' concept of a great voice out front with backup singers who harmonized like angels. In a sense, the Orioles were the very first rock-and-roll band.

In 1955, a young Texan named Joe Arrington, Jr., came onstage a nervous wreck and surprised himself more than anyone else when he left the stage a winner. He lived in a Long Island flophouse and was working for peanuts in a clothing store, but he sang with his buddies on street corners at night. They persuaded him to try the contest. He was totally befuddled when he began his tune, "Woke Up This Morning," but there was power in his pipes. He became one of the stars of sixties soul—Joe Tex.

Until now, every book and newspaper or magazine article written about the Apollo has told the story of how James Brown came out of nowhere to appear on Amateur Night. The legend goes that he was so poor, the stage manager at the time had to lend him shoes and a shirt to wear onstage.

John Davenport was just a seventeen-year-old kid from Detroit when he changed his name to Little Willie John and had his first rhythm and blues hit in 1955. A few years later, Peggy Lee covered one of Willie's tunes and made it an international hit—"Fever." And poor Willie was just a thirty-year-old kid when he died of a fever in prison, where he was sent on a manslaughter conviction after killing a man in a fight.

One of Willie John's dearest friends became the greatest soul man of them all. Here, James Brown, as he appeared in his prime.

The truth is that James had been around for years before he first played the Apollo. It was in the spring of 1959, and James was a professional, with a full band, a well-produced act, and, yes, a complete wardrobe. Perhaps the legend took hold because James and his group were upset because they knew how good they were and it was embarrassing for them to find themselves on the bottom of the bill.

James was in his prime, and he was burning. The audience was in love with him, and at the end of each show the stage was so hot, the next act got burned.

But somebody had it in for James, and he languished there at the bottom of the bill until one night when he threatened to quit. And he did it in a very novel way. At the end of an especially hot set, with the audience screaming for more, James had each member of the band pick up an instrument and carry it offstage—through the audience! James himself led the procession. They marched single-file off the stage and up the center aisle. Before they reached the 125th Street door, James had a new contract saying he would be second from the top of the bill. Only the headliner would come after him. But James was so strong, no headliner wanted to follow him onstage, so he finally got the number-one spot that he deserved.

I always liked the stories about James Brown winning Amateur Night in borrowed clothes. Too bad they weren't true. But what can I tell you? Again—knucklehead historians!

One famous star-to-be who *did* win was a sixteen-year-old gospel singer from East Orange, New Jersey. Dionne Warwick competed in Amateur Night in 1958 with her church group, the Gospel Aires. Dionne, who had never done much singing outside the church, loved the sound of applause from that secular audience so much, she soon decided to become a pop singer.

During the 1950s I had a hand in introducing rock and roll to New York City. I had a live radio show on WOV that broadcast from the Palm Cafe on 125th Street, just off Seventh Avenue. The restaurant management built a big booth for me in a central location in the room, where I did my show. I went out live over the air, spinning platters and interviewing musical guests and VIPs.

There was a Turkish fellow who came around with his partner, a dentist, and these two unlikely characters would check out the talent at the Apollo. They signed up all the young R&B stars and then they'd come up to the Palm and break my door down, asking me to spin their records over the air. They were Ahmet Ertegun, an absolute brain wave whose father was the Turkish ambassador to the United States, and his partner, Dr. Herb Abramson. They formed a little independent company called Atlantic Records in the late 1940s, and they used to hang around Harlem all the time.

Ertegun and Abramson put the groups they heard in Harlem under contract and booked them into studios downtown and tried to capture on record what was happening in the theatres and clubs.

They weren't the only ones who realized the potential of rhythm and blues. The amateur show was a real Mecca for managers, agents, and record-company people. They would wait like vultures in the wings and fall all over one another trying to sign up amateur winners. People like Columbia Records scout John Hammond would show up at the Apollo or the Palm Cafe to check out new acts I might have found. I'd discover talents and Hammond would rediscover them. Hammond's first big claim to fame was that he brought Gene Autry to New York and signed him to a small label that put out ''This Gray Haired Daddy of Mine.'' It was a huge hit. But what John Hammond did best was steal Harlem talent and record it for Columbia.

The big record companies couldn't control everything—far from it. Independent record labels were springing up all over the place to fill the demand for the new black combos that the majors, who were stuck on middle-of-the-road pop, didn't bother with. The many small combos were easy to manage and easy to record: no worries about mikeing a full orchestra or getting fifteen men and their equipment into a studio at the same time. Anybody could record some hot new combo in a garage, and the record could explode. It was a wild time, and to get the fax on wax all you needed was a few hundred dollars to rent some equipment, find a hall, and have a ball.

Besides Atlantic, there were many successful indies: Savoy, Aladdin, Modern, Imperial, Chess, Blue Note, Fury, King, and one on 125th Street called ''Bobby's,'' started by Bobby Robinson, a black record shop entrepreneur. Bobby's store was the size of a cell on Riker's Island, had a shoeshine parlor with two chairs on one side and record racks on the other. He had a sound system rigged up so the latest tunes blasted out onto the street. Then he started recording and became one of the top R&B labels in the country.

If you cruised 125th Street in those days, you would have thought rhythm and blues was the only music in the world. It was all that was heard, and the excitement and energy of that music infected the entire community. R&B was Harlem's own music. It was Harlem's secret. Downtown, it wasn't heard of. Tell people downtown that Ruth Brown and Jimmy Reed were playing the Apollo and they could get in for three dollars and listen to the best R&B in the world, they'd look at you like you had permanent residence at Bellevue.

People never heard R&B because radio wasn't playing it. This music was known as "race music," which meant black music—and white disc jockeys were afraid to play it. I've never been able to understand how a sound can be black or green or yellow. But somebody came up with the idea to segregate "black music," and it caught on. *Billboard* and other magazines still classify music by race: a record's either R&B or pop. If it's a really *hot* R&B record, it "crosses over" to pop, which means it's good enough to be played on so-called white radio. My radio has knobs for "on" and "off" and a dial to switch stations. Nowhere is a button marked "black" or "white."

Years ago, black music was "jungle music," which was judged to be evil. It was supposed to bring out the black devil (and I thought he was red!) in anyone who listened to it. Newspapers, radio, and

Screamin' Jay Hawkins didn't get his name from the way he sang. That was more like a shout. It was the audiences that did the screaming—especially when Jay made his entrance by popping out of a coffin.

Lloyd Price was another great talent out of the Big Easy. Lloyd had an R&B hit with "Lawdy Miss Clawdy" several years before Elvis covered the song. In the late fifties, he turned up on the pop charts with his "Personality."

TV tried to smear rock and roll, saying it incited violence and corrupted youth. Some even said it was a communist plot. I think it was all due to a deep-based fear of sex. Suggestive lyrics had always been a part of the blues—whites were just hearing it for the first time. Yet this controversy is still going on today with the PMRC and disc jockeys who censor lyrics.

Years ago, you'd get run out of a lot of towns for having anything good to say about rhythm and blues. A lot of radio stations wouldn't play it because they were afraid of offending the people who paid their bills and of outraging the community. But I could and did play R&B on my radio show—and the community was swingin' right along with me. I had R&B all to myself. The trouble was, nobody outside Harlem and other black communities around the country would play these "race" records over the radio. The Top 40 was called the hit parade back then, and it was all quiet, sweet music like "How Much Is That Doggie in the Window." There was no Ruth Brown in the hit parade, believe me. Ruth was making great records for Ahmet and Herb, but nobody in the white record-buying world was hearing it, because white radio wasn't playing it.

Of course, I never thought of radio as white radio or black radio. I was just a deejay. And when Ertegun came around with recordings of music by groups who were driving the kids wild at the Apollo, I had to play them. They were great records—fantastic records. Everybody was dancing and rocking along with them; listeners—black and white—would call in and say they wanted to hear more. The big radio stations knew about this music by groups from Harlem. But they assumed that people who listened to the hit parade weren't interested in rhythm and blues. If they were, it would be on the hit parade, wouldn't it? That's the way they thought.

A funny thing happened. Instead of killing rhythm and blues, the lack of airplay gave it an underground mystique. People who couldn't hear it on radio wanted to hear it live. That's why they lined up at the clubs and packed the Apollo every night of the week.

All the while, excitement about the music grew. More and more groups played the new music, getting louder and rawer and whipping crowds into a frenzy. Finally, white singers and groups, such as Elvis, the Beatles, and the Rolling Stones, copied the black sound and conquered the record charts with it.

Another group in the Louis Jordan tradition, the Coasters were Amateur Night winners who went on to a tremendous success with a string of pop hits in the fifties and sixties, including the novelty classic "Charlie Brown."

While most radio deejays were debating about whether it was junk music, I had the privilege of helping to break all these amazing new R&B records—great stuff by artists like Ruth Brown, Fats Domino, Jimmy Reed, Joe Tex, Ray Charles, Sam and Dave, and a host of other great artists. It got the audience hooked. My show got the ratings; we won our time slot every night. So people started wondering, "What's Cooper got going up there at the Palm?"

There was a guy named Teddy Reig, a record producer, who used to come to the Palm every night and listen to my show. He'd go to the station manager and say, "Yeah, man, Coop's really cuttin' it good. I'm diggin' it the most. I want to take these tapes and play 'em back home." It was almost a repeat of what happened with the WMCA Amateur Night broadcasts in the thirties—without my knowing it, the station had recorded our Original Harlem Amateur Night and distributed it to stations all across the country. They syndicated my show. But in those days, there was no such thing as syndication rights, so naturally I never saw a dime.

Then, twenty years later, there I was doing another live radio show, and again it got syndicated without my knowing it.

This character took tapes of my show to Cleveland, where he had a friend on some little station that needed a shot in the arm. So he played the tapes for this Cleveland deejay, a white guy, and the deejay went wild for them. But he couldn't start playing tapes of "The Ralph Cooper Show" on his own show in Cleveland. So he took my concept, my format, my playlist, and my raps and called it "The Moondog Show," which became a huge success. He didn't want anybody to know that he was playing rhythm and blues "race records."

Etta James answered Hank Ballard's sexy and suggestive R&B hit, "Work with Me, Annie," by singing "Roll with Me, Henry." But it was Georgia Gibbs's sanitized, white-bread version of Etta's classic—Gibbs changed the title to "Dance with Me, Henry"— that made the hit parade.

One of the greatest doo-wop groups, the Five Satins showed off their silky-smooth vocals in their biggest hit, "In the Still of the Night."

So he took a phrase that had been used in black music for years, which was slang for doin' it: "rock and roll."

That deejay, of course, was named Alan Freed, and he's now known as the Father of Rock and Roll, and it's because of him that the Rock and Roll Hall of Fame is being built in Cleveland, Ohio. Now I don't want to start a rumble, but it seems to me that museum should be built in Harlem. But Cleveland? Because Alan Freed once heard rhythm-and-blues records from Ralph Cooper's Show Live at the Palm? I'm sure Cleveland has many, many enthusiastic rock-and-roll fans who were able to convince the Hall of Fame committee that rock and roll began in Cleveland. But I'm afraid the same thing happened that has happened so often in the cultural history of our country: racist thinking entered into the decision.

Alan Freed performed the same function Elvis Presley performed, though he didn't do it as well. Alan Freed and Elvis both claimed the legacy of rock and roll for whites. They both gave rock and roll a white face, even though the music has a black soul.

To me, Elvis Presley is a great rhythm-and-blues singer who happens to be white. Sam Phillips said he wanted a white man who sounded black. He said he would be a billionaire if he could find "a white man with the Negro sound." That's a famous detail of rock-and-roll history that black people have always found a bit offensive. But Sam Phillips was just telling it like it is. And everybody knows he was right. Sam Cooke may have been a better singer than Elvis, but in those days, when Jim Crow still cast its shadow over America, Sam could never have become as big a star. Maybe today he could. Who's bigger than Michael Jackson? Though Michael is doing his best to look like somebody who would have met Sam Phillips's requirements in 1954.

To me, the truth of what Sam Phillips was saying is proven by Otis Blackwell. Otis is one of the most gifted rock-and-roll composers ever. He sang and wrote a golden string of tunes that became the biggest and best rock-and-roll records ever recorded: "Don't Be Cruel," "All Shook Up," "Great Balls of Fire." Otis Blackwell is the King of Rock and Roll Songwriters. But he's not living in any Graceland. The reason Otis Blackwell isn't a famous star is that the world never heard him sing his own songs, even though they heard his lyrics, his melodies, his arrangements, his instrumentation, his vocal style. And that was because Elvis and Jerry Lee Lewis recorded Otis's songs exactly as Otis wrote them. They copied his demo records note for note, right down to the "oo-oo-oo"'s and the stops and starts in "Don't Be Cruel" and the wild-man squealing in "Great Balls of Fire."

But Otis, who used to perform at the Apollo and who had some minor hits of his own, sold the rights to his greatest songs to Moe Gale for twenty-five dollars each. He walked into the Brill Building on Broadway and sold "Don't Be Cruel" and five other songs for a hundred and fifty dollars, enough to pay the rent on his Harlem apartment. Who knows how many copies of "Don't Be Cruel" have sold throughout the world in the last thirty years? I think it's one of the best rock-and-roll songs of all time. But Otis didn't even get all the royalties. Presley got half of all Otis's tunes, because Elvis's manager, Colonel Tom Parker, told Otis, "Either give Elvis cowriting credit or he ain't gonna do your song, boy." Of course, half of a five-million seller is better than nothing. Still and all, I don't know how Otis feels about it, but it sure as hell irks me to pick up one of Presley's million-selling records and look at the songwriting credit and read "Presley-Blackwell." They even gave Elvis top billing!

Just about all of Elvis's early rock-and-roll hits were written, arranged, and first performed by black artists. His first hit in the South was "Lawdy Miss Clawdy," written by Arthur "Big Boy" Crudup and recorded earlier by Lloyd Price. Even "Hound Dog," the song that made him famous, was a hit on the black rhythm-and-blues charts by Big Mama Thornton. Elvis just copied it, note for note. He used Big Mama's arrangement; he used the same tempo, the same inflections, the same everything. There's no telling how much Elvis owed Big Mama Thornton.

That's the history of rock and roll. Ruth Brown's biggest-selling song was "Mama, He Treats Your Daughter Mean." But Tony Bennett copied her song and it went to the top of the hit parade. Pat Boone is a nice man, but he couldn't sing his way out of his own shower. Yet Pat Boone's milquetoast cover of Fats Domino's "Ain't That a Shame" sold more copies than Fats's original, and it made Boone a helluva lot more money than Fats ever saw, even with the writer's royalties.

The history of American popular music is chock-full of these inequities. It didn't start with Elvis and Otis and Big Mama. Best-selling white covers of songs first written and performed by black artists are as old as "Swing Low, Sweet Chariot." A big band in the 1940s called the Sunset Royals was famous for its arrangements of "Marie," "On the Sunny Side of the Street," and "Sweet Sue." Each of those arrangements was taken from the Royals and recorded note for note by Tommy Dorsey's band and became a huge hit. Dorsey became rich and famous. But who's heard of the Sunset Royals? People have been getting fabulously wealthy by "covering" other peo-

Ruth Brown won Amateur Night in the forties and returned as an R&B star in the fifties. One of the first artists signed by Atlantic Records, which became known as "the house that Ruth built," she had a string of million-selling singles. But Ruth spent the sixties cleaning houses on Long Island in order to put her children through school. In 1989, Ruth won a Tony Award for her role in *Black and Blue*, the smash Broadway hit inspired by the musical revues popular at the Apollo and on other Harlem stages in the twenties and thirties.

ple's songs for generations. And it's still happening. Even now they get tricked left and right. Little Richard sold the rights to all his greatest hits years ago due to economics. Ruth Brown is just now getting her due and even won a Tony Award for a Broadway vehicle *Black and Blue,* a tribute to Harlem show business. But for years Ruth struggled to make ends meet, even though in the fifties she sold millions of records for Atlantic.

Ruth, whose biggest hits were "covered" by white performers for the hit parade, started out on my Amateur Night in Harlem show. Ironically, she sang a Bing Crosby song, "It Could Happen to You"—but she didn't sing it like Der Bingle. The audience was so blown away, they called her back to repeat the chorus. Ruth went on to sell so many records for Ahmet and Herb, they called Atlantic Records "the House That Ruth Built." But in the sixties, she was reduced to working as a maid on Long Island, cleaning floors and scrubbing toilet bowls. I'd bet anything the people who hired her didn't know or care that they were living in "Houses That Ruth Cleaned."

Ruth is finally getting a settlement for back royalties. But Ahmet and Herb weren't doing anything different than any other record company. They charged artists for tour costs, so that after six months of one-night stands, Ruth came home and asked for her royalties and the record company handed her a bill: so much for hired cars, so much for costumes, so much for hotels—so much money *she* owed *them* in the end. It was the same thing that happened to Ma Rainey forty years before.

Now Atlantic has agreed to look into back royalty payments for Sam and Dave and a number of other R&B artists. Still, a twenty-thousand dollar settlement doesn't seem like much to me. Ruth did a hell of a lot for them. She sold millions of records. There's no telling how much she earned for them. I should have 10 percent of what she earned for Atlantic—just 10 percent and I'd be able to retire rich in Hawaii.

Remember Little Eva Boyd? She worked as baby-sitter for two Tin Pan Alley rock-and-roll writers, Carole King and Gerry Goffin. They wrote a song called "The Loco-Motion" and they asked her to sing it. Eva was another church singer, and they heard her sing to their baby and knew she was good.

She sang "The Loco-Motion" and they loved it. The record company put it out and Little Eva became a star. She was booked on a string of rock-and-roll package tours that traveled all over the country. But Eva's was the same story as Ruth Brown's and Ma Rainey's and the rest. When she got back home to the Bronx, she wanted to take her money and buy her mama a house and go to college. But there wasn't any money. Little Eva stayed in show business right on through the sixties and seventies. But she might as well have gone back to babysitting, because now she's living in South Carolina, where

Tina Turner only had eyes for Ike in the late fifties, when this was the powerhouse couple's preferred publicity shot—before they crossed over into pop.

her people are from. She's a working mother on welfare. She works in a barbeque kitchen as a cook.

Last year Kylie Minogue, a soap-opera actress from Australia, released an almost note-for-note cover of "The Loco-Motion." But instead of the great saxophone parts in Little Eva's version, they used a synthesizer. And Kylie's voice isn't as full as Eva's. The new "Loco-Motion" was a watered-down version, as "sanitized" as anything Pat Boone covered in the 1950s. And it sold millions of copies—which makes Carole King very happy but does nothing for Eva Boyd.

Eventually artists got smart. They said, "I'm not cutting that record without money up front." So the record companies said,

It's impossible to name all the great, half-forgotten stars from the glory years of R&B. But among them were...Sweet Georgia Brown. Whenever I saw her, I couldn't help singing her name....

...and Gloria Lynne, another amateur who sang like a pro the night she won Amateur Night. Later she was in a group called the Dorsey Sisters....

"Fine, here's a thousand-dollar advance." The singer takes the money, and that's the last thousand he'll ever see from that record. He'll owe that thousand dollars forever.

It's like my brother, Walter, bless him. He once gave my daughter Lisa ten dollars when she was a little girl. Then, any time she wanted something, she would tell me, "Dad, I need a dollar. As soon as I get my ten changed, I'll pay you back." She worked me for at least a hundred dollars off that ten before she got it changed.

That practice of show-business sharecropping we talked about in the 1920s and 1930s existed right on through the fifties and sixties. A bitterness still exists among many performers to this day—a bitterness from the theft of their songs, their sound, their talent.

Look at Bo Diddley. He's still fighting in court to get the rights to the Bo Diddley beat that's been used by every rock-and-roll musician in the business, from Buddy Holly to the Rolling Stones and George Thorogood. Bo admits he's bitter.

Same with Little Richard. Pat Boone owns the rights to some of Richard's compositions. That means every time someone sings it, Pat Boone gets paid for it, not Richard.

It was hard as hell for Richard to see Elvis Presley and the Beatles take his numbers and make their fortunes and all the while Richard, who created those songs, gets nothing. It's still a form of show-business sharecropping. You work the land, but you don't own it; you invent the sound, but you can't profit from it.

Granted, many artists were seduced by the lure of fast money. That hundred and fifty must have seemed like a lot of money to Otis Blackwell. And as bad and sad a thing as that is, the bottom line is he never should have sold those songs for a song.

Today, the rip-offs aren't so prevalent. You still have white acts "borrowing" from black acts, but it's usually in the form of new covers of old songs. In the old days, big-name black acts would appear at the Apollo and a white act would come in and just copy whatever they did. It was not unheard of for one group to get another group's demo recording and submit it to the record company as their own. Then they'd rerecord it using the same arrangement and sound and it would be a big hit.

But everything comes around. Yesterday, the Beatles covered Little Richard and Chuck Berry. Today, Michael Jackson covers the Beatles. Hell, Michael owns the entire Beatles catalogue. He's even singing Beatles songs in his concerts and releasing them as singles. Isn't that something?

Yesterday, radio stations wouldn't play music by black artists because they were afraid of losing advertising. Today, Madison Avenue lives by black music. It seems every commercial is a Motown black-music video. People don't realize that when "Murphy Brown" opens with a great old soul song from the sixties, the artist who created it probably does not have a condo on Easy Street. Chances are he's got no record contract and he's out on the road playing one-night stands in order to make the rent.

In 1956 I decided to branch out once again and try something new. I had performed in all the great theatres and headlined in many of them. I had been to Hollywood and wrote, produced, and starred in several films. I had two shows on radio, and both were successful. So I decided to see if my luck would hold on television. I called the show "Spotlight on Harlem" and patterned it after my Amateur Night show. But instead of having people sit to dig the tunes at the Apollo, I invited people to come into the ABC studios on Sixty-sixth Street.

One day I was walking down the street and there was a group of kids on the corner doing the doo-wop. The leader of the group was a mere child. But this little boy had a fantastic voice. I walked past dozens of street singers every week in those days, but this group stopped me dead in my tracks. I thought, "Man, this is too good to be true." I talked to the leader, the young kid, and he surprised me by calling me Mr. Cooper. It turned out he knew me because he had performed on Amateur Night as a drummer for a group called the Esquires. So I invited him and his group to audition for "Spotlight on Harlem." They were great singers, and I made a spot for them on the next show.

The show was done live on Saturday night, and right after it aired, I got calls from four or five different record companies wanting to sign Frankie Lymon and the Teenagers. "Why Do Fools Fall in Love?" was the Teenagers' biggest hit, though they had many before Frankie's voice changed. He died broke, and tragically, from a heroin overdose, when he was only twenty-six.

My "Harlem Spotlite" variety television show on New York's Channel 13 was a precursor to Ed Sullivan's show. Our live broadcast beat all competition in its time slot.

RALPH COOPER'S

HARLEM SPOTLITE

Morris Levy, who owned Birdland and a record label called Roulette Records, was the man who first signed Frankie. He was another of the small independent businessmen who realized the cash potential of rhythm and blues and rock and roll. Morris's wife was an artists' manager who had another former Amateur Night winner under contract, a struggling New York singer named Harry Belafonte. All Harry did was sing love ballads, and he was going nowhere slow. Morris's wife talked him into taking a vacation in Jamaica. Now I can talk to a Jamaican all day long and not understand a word he says. But Harry's parents were Jamaican, and as soon as he got down there, he fell

Little Anthony Gourdine couldn't pass our amateur auditions he was so nervous. But he and his Imperials later became a big hit at the Apollo. (What does "Shimmy shimmy cocoa puff" mean, anyway?)

THE NEW SENSATION

Betti Mays and her Swing-Tette

Exclusive Tour Direction

Ralph Cooper

307 LENOX AVE., NEW YORK, ●MOnument 2-6322

I used to wear more hats than Sinatra. When I wasn't busy hosting Amateur Night at the Apollo or "Spotlite," or working as emcee in various clubs around town, or doing my duty as one of New York's leading radio deejays, I found time to own and operate my own booking and management agencies. I even did some copywriting. Note Miss Mays's "oomphy gowns." What do you suppose I meant by that?

in love with the place. He took up with a folk artist who taught him the dialect and introduced him to the island music. He was a natural! Harry limboed onto a local work song: ''Workin' the banana boat all day long . . .'' Tall, handsome, and talented, Harry came back to New York and became the new sensation singing ''Day-O.''

In those years, besides doing my radio and TV gigs, I worked as a booking agent for the Gale Agency packaging tours. I also performed some and still managed to find time to host the amateur show at the Apollo.

Even though the kind of show business I had grown up in was disappearing, so much was happening so fast, I didn't have time for nostalgia. Who could pine for the past with all that screaming going on? Anyway, in show business, it's never a good idea to stand still and look back; you never know what might be ready to pass you by. And in the 1950s, the future was coming on fast.

Here's Betti in the gown that inspired the ad.

9

Soul City

★ ★

For the Apollo Theatre, for black show business itself, and for me, the sixties were the best of times and the worst of times and, for a while, the most tragic of times. By the middle of the decade, the Apollo had begun to be hurt by its own success. In the early years of R&B, the theatre was sold out almost every night as the greatest singing sensations in popular music took the stage and audiences by storm. But the Apollo's wonderful secret got out. The great soul stars that the theatre first projected to the world became so successful Harlem couldn't afford them. Labor problems that had loomed over the theatre for decades now threatened to explode. Schiffman's arrogant attitude was no longer tolerated by workers forced to toil long hours for meager wages in woeful working conditions. The theatre's problems were magnified by its popularity. The Apollo's biggest stars were finally achieving fame in their own right, not as sharecroppers working the musical fields for absentee managers but as stars—bright, shining, and free.

Yet in another sense, Aretha Franklin, Smokey Robinson, James Brown, Otis Redding, Wilson Pickett, Sam and Dave, the Supremes, the Four Tops, the Temptations, Marvin Gaye, and all the top soul singers and vocal groups of the era still rode in the back of the show-business bus. The best seats went to groups such as the Beatles and the Rolling Stones, whose expert re-recording of songs by black

Believe it or not, Ray Charles didn't have his first hit until 1959. That's when the "Soul Genius" released "What'd I Say," a crossover hit no one dared cover.

rhythm-and-blues groups made Sam Phillips's notion of a wedding between white artists and the "black sound" seem downright prophetic.

For me, the whole world collapsed when I was stricken by what the doctors said was a career-ending illness. But as often happens, when one door closed, another opened—onto a challenging world that was almost, but not quite, as exciting.

At the same time as I watched the Apollo begin its decline and faced the very real possibility that I would never perform onstage again, I lost a very close and valued friend. I first met Malcolm Little at the Elks' Rendezvous at which time he was a waiter—very studious and sincere. Years later I renewed my friendship with the now Malcolm X backstage at the Apollo Theatre. It ended a few short years later when Malcolm X, as he was known to his legions of followers, was gunned down. How I became not an eyewitness but an "ear witness" to one of the most horrifying political murders in Harlem history is a story you will hear soon.

But first the good news. For many years, soul music was a Harlem secret. Soul was the ultimate blend of rhythm and blues and gospel—a funky groove that swung on the fence between the sensuous and the spiritual, the sacred and secular. Soul singers were like preachers, shouting and soothing and wooing their flocks. Every night the Apollo was rocking with James Brown's exuberant, cape-swirling showmanship; Sam Cooke was sending them to heaven with his heart-melting love songs; Aretha Franklin was putting gospel passion behind some earthy anthems; Dinah Washington, the Queen, was flipping them out with her sexy blues. You had to stand in line for hours and hours to get tickets to some of those shows. But outside Harlem, it was still "Who is James Brown?" "The Apollo? I thought that went out with vaudeville." "What did Sam cook?" Downtown, people were still not hip to the trip. They thought "out of sight" was a condition of the blind.

With the advent of black disc jockeys, radio commenced playing the black artist. Acts that had headlined the Apollo for three dollars at the door, the Apollo could now no longer afford. Here's a for-instance: Three brothers from Cincinnati won an Amateur Night contest in the late fifties. Within a year, the Isley Brothers—Kelly, Rudolph, and Ronald—came back as professionals, and soon after, they were headlining for two thousand dollars a week. That was for all three brothers, plus their band. They did twenty-eight shows for the week for that two thousand dollars. Then, in 1959, something happened: "Shout." It was a huge single that crossed over. "You make me want to SHOUT!"—that was one rave tune. Every teenager in America bought that single—black teenagers and white teenagers. The Isleys followed with "Twist and Shout" three years later. You didn't have a party or a sock hop in 1962 unless you played "Twist

I don't know why Chubby Checker's note-for-note cover and not Hank Ballard's original version of his party song "The Twist" became one of the biggest-selling single records of all time. Chubby was a fine talent in his own right. And his may have been the first case of black singer hitting with a pop "cover" of another black performer's song. Music buffs might be interested to know that the dance step that inspired Hank to write "The Twist" was created by the guys in his band, the Midnighters.

and Shout." That too was a hot side, a happenin' platter. It went through the roof.

Now that the Isleys hit, they became a thirty-five-thousand-dollar-a-night-against-percentages act. Some people thought, "Oh, man, the Isleys—they're too busy playing the Copa to mess with the old uptown scene." But they didn't stop playing the Apollo because they thought they were too good. The fact was that no theatre in Harlem could afford the Isley Brothers once they broke big. The Apollo sure couldn't and the Apollo was *it* in Harlem by that time. All the other theatres were in decline, about to take early retirement without the benefits.

Still, the Apollo was happening. If you don't have the money for steak, go for the eggs—which was why Ralph Cooper's Amateur Night was so vital. The theatre survived by booking smaller acts and discovering new talent, which is exactly what Amateur Night did. The Jackson 5, the Shirelles, Gladys Knight, Patti LaBelle, and Wilson Pickett were all Amateur Night winners who worked their way up to

One of Motown's greatest singers and songwriters, Smokey Robinson performed Miracles.

become headliners at the Apollo. As long as there were Michael Jacksons and Gladys Knights out there waiting to be discovered, the theatre was okay. Leslie Uggams was a pretty little pre-teen when she won her first Amateur Night. She won week after week. She waited to make her real career move when she was an elderly and sweet sixteen.

Ronnie Spector was a young girl who lived down the street when she got her start one Wednesday at the Apollo. She was like family: her dad owned a sandwich shop next door to the theatre, and she lived in the Grant Projects on 125th Street. Her name in those days was Veronica Bennett, and she rounded up one of her sisters and a

Until the Supremes came along, the Shirelles were the greatest of the "girl groups." The gals, who sold millions of copies of their hits "Soldier Boy" and "Dedicated to the One I Love," got their start on Amateur Night.

The tall fellow (*second from the right*) is Teddy Pendergrass, with his old group, Harold Melvin and the Blue Notes.

cousin to sing with her and they became the Ronettes because Ronnie had the best voice—otherwise they might have been the Estellettes or the Nedraettes. They came to Amateur Night and won first place. Then Phil Spector married Ronnie and made the Ronettes the premiere girl group. Poor Ronnie must have wished she was back on 125th Street when Phil went weird on her a few years later and wouldn't let her leave his Beverly Hills mansion.

The Apollo thrived on finding young talent like the Ronettes. The theatre needed new acts because the big established groups were finding they could make more money in one night at Madison Square Garden than they could make in fifteen weeks at the Apollo. Economically, the Apollo put itself out of business. We could seat fewer than fifteen hundred people, which meant we couldn't pay an act forty thousand dollars, or thirty thousand dollars, or even twenty-five thousand dollars, which by the late sixties was cheap for a big-name group. It was ironic, since those acts were able to command that kind of money because they started out playing for smart, enthusiastic audiences four shows a day for a week at a time—a grueling schedule that forced acts to hone their craft razor-sharp. The up-and-comers played with a hunger to be reckoned with: Smokey's Miracles, the Supremes, the Jackson 5. They all did the twenty-eight-shows-a-week grind, established their acts on these boards, launched their stars from the Apollo stage. But once the big money came in, bye-bye first love.

When the Jackson 5 won Amateur Night, it seemed like only a week passed before they were priced out of our range. Soon the Jacksons were so big, they would only come back and play the Apollo for old times' sake, almost as a benefit for the theatre where it all began for them.

Michael was just a little bitty boy, maybe five or six years old, when the Jackson 5 started out in Gary, Indiana. By the time he was nine, he and his brothers had won every talent show and amateur contest in the Midwest. They'd even been to Chicago and made a name for themselves there. People said the big record companies would be calling any day now. But Joe Jackson, the boys' father, insisted the band had to play the Apollo's amateur show. If they could make it there, he knew, the Jackson 5 would make it anywhere. Michael was ten when the family drove to New York for the Wednesday-night show, which they won in a walk. A producer from David Frost's TV show was in the audience, and when the boys got back to Gary, there was an offer from Frost to appear on his show.

As far as the boys were concerned, national TV exposure was all they needed. But before the Frost date, something even bigger came along: an audition at Motown Records in Detroit. Just a few weeks after winning Amateur Night in Harlem, Michael and his brothers got a contract from Motown, and their destiny was signed, sealed, and delivered.

For the next few years, the Jackson 5 were the biggest thing in popular music. The group was a favorite of the Apollo audience, and the feeling was mutual, because the boys thought of the Apollo stage as the platform that launched their career. Marlon Jackson says he learned two lessons at the Apollo: ''Don't do drugs and don't get a big head.'' In his autobiography, *Moonwalker,* Michael remembers

Leslie Uggams (*below left*), an abundance of talent, was just eight years old when she won her first Amateur Night contest. Melissa Morgan (*top left*), Phyllis Hyman, and (*below right*) the great Eartha Kitt.

standing in the thick folds of the theatre's "smelly" old curtain, watching Jackie Wilson, the O'Jays, and especially James Brown. Michael must have studied every move James ever made. He learned how to move and sing and breathe and electrify, as well as moonwalk, at the Apollo.

The only other person I knew who hung out at the Apollo on a regular basis who was even younger than Michael was my own son, Ralph II. From the time he was about four years old, I took Ralph with me everywhere. We were like a team. He would traipse around behind me wherever I went. He made all the restaurants, he met all the stars, he knew all the maître d's and club owners. He often stayed up late—to his mother's discontent, it's true, but he got one helluva good education. Backstage at the Apollo or in the sound booth at the radio station or in the television studio—these places were Ralph's school. I must add that Ralph did attend Fieldston School in Riverdale and graduated from the prestigious Birch Wathen School in Manhattan before attending Elizabeth Seton College and City College of New York. So life wasn't all show business for Ralph—but almost.

There were still good times to be had in Harlem in the sixties, but it wasn't one cookin' time after another like it had been in past years. It was as if the good times weren't having a great time. Poverty at home and war overseas had a lot to do with it. Local boys were getting drafted because they were poor; they got sent to 'Nam because they didn't have the college deferments. That made for a lot of sadness and anger in Harlem.

There was strong opposition to the war in Harlem. Once Martin Luther King himself laid out how he felt, people took up the fight against the fighting. Many agreed with Muhammad Ali, who said us black folks got no fight with yellow folks. When Eartha Kitt sang at the White House, people got upset because she spoke her mind about the war. That was a brave thing for her to do. You don't get a gig singing for the President of the United States every day. And nobody wants to offend the Man. You don't bad-mouth the club owner when you play his room; when you do a wedding, don't put down the groom. But Eartha spoke her mind to President Johnson, and it caused a helluva stir. There was a boycott against her. She couldn't get a booking in Biloxi within a week of that White House mess. As a result, one of the great singers of the age could not play a date in the United States, the home of free speech, because she exercised her right to speak out. I didn't think this was right. So I got some people together to back a concert at the Apollo and we got Eartha Kitt to headline. Eartha was a big hit, of course, and that event put her back on the road. It ended the boycott—nobody wanted to pass up a chance to book a talent who could sell out the Apollo Theatre.

Things were changing in Harlem in the 1960s. The life seemed to be draining out of the community. There was less romance, less excitement; more poverty, more despair. Some of it was the result of tragedy: riots and urban decay and hard drugs took their toll.

But the positive energies were missing, too. Theatres were dark; small clubs were shutting down. The grand and beautiful restaurants were going bust or moving to better locations. Without the nightlife and the show people and the excitement they create, it was easier for negative forces to get the upper hand.

One of the greats, Bobby "Blue" Bland helped keep the blues alive long enough for its sixties revival.

There were still good times, of course. After work, performers would make the scene at Creole Pete's, which was located across from the Lafayette Theatre, on Seventh Avenue at 132nd Street. Louis Armstrong, Nipsey Russell, Baron Wilson, my good friend, all sorts of people used to meet at Pete's. We'd show up at four in the morning after the clubs closed and wouldn't get home till ten or eleven. Pete cooked some beautiful gumbo, and if we weren't hungry for that, we'd go over to Ribs in the Rough, which was a joint Sidney Poitier owned at 127th and Seventh.

Nipsey and our good friend Baron Wilson and I liked to meet at Hamburger Heaven on Park Avenue at Fifty-seventh Street downtown. We were all there having an early-morning breakfast when Tommy Dorsey came in. Tommy and his brother Jimmy had a show on network television. They were the summer replacement for Jackie Gleason. We stayed late that morning, reminiscing with Tommy, talking about the old days at the Savoy Ballroom and the Apollo when he and his brother would come up to Harlem to catch the hot new acts. We had a great time together. We must have talked for two hours.

When I got up the next afternoon, I turned on the radio to catch the news: "Bandleader Tommy Dorsey is dead." I thought Baron was in the next room pulling some kind of joke. I couldn't believe it! But it was cold truth. Dorsey had gone home to bed and choked to death. I don't know how or what happened. But it was frightening. And sad. Somehow, it meant that those good times we'd been talking about that night really were gone for good. If Tommy could die just like that, nothing was permanent.

I worked with a lot of people who knew Ed Sullivan. He was a genuinely lovable guy, a nice guy. But he was difficult to do a show with—especially for a comic. He'd stand next to you, stiff as a corpse. I'd bet even Eddie Murphy couldn't get a rise out of him.

Sullivan wasn't the most enlightened emcee in the world. Every black act he had on his show was introduced as "Harlem's own." They could be from Cleveland, Birmingham, Tuscaloosa. It didn't matter to Ed Sullivan. They were always "Harlem's own."

When the Beatles came to this country to appear on the Sullivan show, I was working as a deejay at WHOM, in the midnight to three a.m. slot. It wasn't drive time; it was jive time. I played a lot of R&B and the better rock and roll, so I played a few Beatles songs on my show. There was no great resentment among black listeners to the

Beatles, because they sounded so good. They wrote smart, infectious songs that a lot of black acts covered for themselves, and their singing was in the black style they emulated. You could tell by listening to John Lennon sing that he grew up on black music. He sang with a passion you didn't hear in many white singers.

All the deejays in town were invited down to the Plaza Hotel to meet the Beatles. It was a wild scene, with thousands of white kids down in the street and these skinny young men, who didn't seem much older than the kids below, up in the suites, bewildered by the frenzy going on around them. I was introduced to the group, and one of them—I'm not sure which—said, " 'Ello, mate, I've heard your show. You play great music." The accent was a surprise to me, because on record they sounded black. These were very charismatic young men. They wanted to know all about the Apollo Theatre. They were artists who wanted to pay tribute to the source.

I thought that maybe they really *had* heard my show, because I was still one of the only deejays in New York who was playing true rock and roll, R&B, and soul. Every other deejay in the room was playing Top 40, which in those days was Chuck Berry songs sung by Johnny Rivers. Now Johnny is a nice guy and I love his song "Poor Side of Town," but when he sings "Maybelline"—well, as Lloyd Bentsen would say, he's no Chuck Berry.

My show was popular among all audiences—black, white, and Chinese—because I had gimmicks and freebies. I'd give away albums and tickets to the Apollo. We took requests, and I had a bank of ten phones that were always flashing. One night I said, "I've got a pair of tickets to the Beatles concert tomorrow night for anybody who can tell me who's buried in Grant's Tomb."

The phones went crazy. Callers said things like, "That's stupid. Grant's buried in Grant's Tomb." "Sorry, wrong answer," we'd say, and hang up before the caller started cussing.

Finally, after two hours of phone calls, a young girl got it right. "Mr. *and Mrs.* Grant are buried in Grant's Tomb." "We got a winner," I said, and she screamed like I'd given her a million dollars.

I hate to say it, but as the sixties progressed, the Apollo declined to the point of decay. Conditions inside the musty old theatre were atrocious—so bad you'd think they were trying to emulate the TOBA. This state of affairs created a lot of bitterness and tension backstage.

The theatre was so run-down it posed a clear danger. There were accidents. Pipes leaked; puddles would develop; people were zapped by electric shocks backstage. There was no decent carpeting on the stairs; performers were always taking tumbles. There was little heat in winter, no air conditioning in summer. The dressing rooms were as depressing as dungeon jail cells. The plaster was falling out of the ceilings; there was no paint.

At one point in the mid-sixties, Sammy Davis, Jr., who was born just fifteen blocks north of the theatre, was making a triumphant return appearance at the Apollo. He wanted to return to Harlem and play the theatre that meant most to him. When his advance people came to the theatre and saw the shameful conditions, they said to Schiffman, "Listen, you're going to have to get these dressing rooms fixed up for Sammy. Nobody should be made to work in this squalor. These dressing rooms are an insult to the history of this great theatre." Sammy's dressing room was quickly spiffed up, but the rest continued to rot as usual. The owners didn't care. They didn't have to spend half their lives in those dressing rooms. They didn't have to use toilets that were always stopped up and overflowing. They didn't have to sweat buckets in summer and shiver all night in winter. They went home to Westchester, sat by the fire, and figured how to squeeze another dollar in profits.

The theatre's deterioration can be seen in a famous photograph of Smokey Robinson teaching the Temptations the words to his latest composition, "My Girl," before going onstage at the Apollo. It's a truly extraordinary photograph, because it captures an important moment in the history of popular music. Here's one of the greatest pop composers of all time teaching the Temps the song that would make them famous—it's probably the best-known of all Motown songs. In the photo you can almost hear Smokey sing, "I got sunshine on a cloudy day/When it's cold outside, I got the month of May." What you can also see is a room that looks like the men's room in a subway station. The bare cement walls are chipped and stained. There's a slab of plywood where the window should be. There's an iron bar over the wood; the plaster is falling off the wall, and the old steam pipes are corroded with rust. The room looks like it was designed for punishment, rather than a sanctuary for performers whose lives are dedicated to bringing pleasure. In his autobiography, Smokey says, "There's no greater feeling in the world than hitting the stage of the

Apollo on the heels of a hit.'' But there's no mention in the book about what a sickening feeling it is to return to those same four depressing fly-specked walls after leaving the stage on a wave of applause. I don't believe even Smokey could have imagined the month of May sitting in that cell on a cold, damp day.

For the crew, conditions were worse. The performers got to leave after a week or a two-week run. But the crew members were virtual prisoners of the theatre's economics. Frank Schiffman ran the theatre like a company store. Crew people were paid so little they had to depend on trying to borrow a hundred dollars every month in order to make the rent. They were so deeply in debt to the theatre, they'd need a money ladder ten stories high to get out.

Before the decade was over, things began to turn against Frank Schiffman. There was enormous pressure from people in the community who were fighting to build black entrepreneurship on 125th Street. Even this late in the game, there were very few black-owned enterprises there. And the Apollo was the most famous of all the businesses on 125th Street.

To resist the pressures raining down on him, Schiffman became active in the Chamber of Commerce, which was still all-white in Harlem. He also became a life member of the NAACP and the Urban League. He made friends and lined up support in the state assembly and various civic organizations.

But then the black nationalists, led by a black historian named Louis Micheaux, began to picket the theatre. They said some of the bookings—one gay production of ''Jewel Box Revue'' in particular—were morally unclean. Then they took up the issue of conditions within the theatre itself, where they found a different kind of ''unclean.'' The nationalists got out on the picket lines every day and told the world that the Apollo was unclean. It was a dirty theatre, unhealthy for workers, performers, and audience members alike. The nationalists boldly blamed the white owner for not caring about the black people who were his customers and workers. Relentless as they were in picketing the theatre, they did have some precedent to follow. A decade earlier, the Apollo chorus girls picketed the theatre to demand a pay increase, which they won. And more recently, Bubba Kinard and I had helped win a settlement under which the stagehands were allowed to join the International Alliance of Theatrical Stage Employees union.

A bright light in a dark decade, Gladys Knight, her brother, and a couple of cousins—including one named Pip—drove up from Georgia to win Amateur Night in 1965.

In response to the nationalist pickets, the theatre closed for two weeks to make alterations. But the changes were all cosmetic—a paint job in the hallways, some new curtains. Conditions had not improved in any essential way. There were still rusted pipes, broken windows, faulty wiring.

This was the beginning of the end for Schiffman. But I don't think he cared that much. When he died, in 1974, he left a legacy I don't intend to glorify.

Schiffman had trouble getting along with all those who refused to kowtow to him. One week he attempted to cancel Johnny Mathis, who was a big star, because Johnny had said something Schiffman didn't like. But Johnny was too big a star for Schiffman to push around. He also tried to cancel Baron Wilson once because he didn't like a joke he was telling onstage. It was a joke that appealed to black people, but Schiffman didn't see the humor in it, and he instructed Baron not to use the joke. I was producing that particular show, and I had to tell Schiffman that he had no business censoring a comedian's material just because he didn't understand it. I told him that canceling Baron Wilson was out of the question. "Either Baron goes on or there will be no show." So Schiffman had to agree.

Schiffman offended a lot of black performers and crew people because of his imperious manner. He talked fast and he liked to talk down to people. He used the King's English in a pretentious way around people who obviously felt uncomfortable because of it. You could always tell: the more elegant in his speech he became, the more he looked down upon the person he was talking to.

I remember seeing Nipsey Russell for the first time at the Baby Grand, on 125th Street. I immediately went to Schiffman and told him about this wonderful new comic I'd seen. Schiffman scoffed: "He's playing a local nightclub. We only hire high-class talent for the Apollo." I told Schiffman, whose regular emcee hadn't showed up for work that week, that Nipsey would be perfect for the job. But Schiffman wouldn't listen. I said, "All right, then, I'll make you a deal. Put Nipsey on the first show. If he doesn't kill 'em I'll fill in for him at the salary you're paying him as a newcomer." Schiffman agreed. Nipsey opened the next show, and he wowed the audience and he wowed Schiffman. He opened with a poem, as usual:

I was out in the backyard one beautiful day, I said to my mother,
"Mama, why don't I have no sisters or no brothers?"
She said, "Go away, go play, don't worry your mother dear.
As lazy as your father was, you're lucky that you got here."

The audience loved it, and Schiffman booked Nipsey—soon to be nicknamed "Harlem's Son of Fun" by the Apollo crowd—for another week. Another career was jump-started by the Apollo.

★　★　★

Despite all the tension inside and the controversy outside, the fabled Apollo still lured talent and audiences. People like Muhammad Ali and Martin Luther King knew they could come in, take a bow, and meet the people. Even Nelson Rockefeller saw the power of the Apollo's legend; one day a mutual friend, Jackie Robinson (the first black in major league baseball), asked me to help him tap into that power.

It was Rockefeller's last campaign for governor, and he was having trouble winning reelection. The polls all showed him behind, and he realized that the black vote in Harlem was crucial to his victory. Jackie Robinson was doing some public relations work for Rocky in those days, and he came to me and said Rocky was the underdog in this race. I know it was hard for a lot of people—especially poor people—to believe that Nelson Rockefeller, a billionaire several times over, could be an underdog. People didn't really think he had any interest in the black community at all. But I knew that the Rockefellers were great philanthropists and had done a lot for the black community. When Jackie asked me to write a proposal outlining some creative ideas for the governor's campaign, I agreed. They set me up in a suite of offices at the Hilton Hotel with a secretary and I wrote up a whole book of ideas, most of which the governor approved. One of them was to go on a walking tour of Harlem.

On the last day of the campaign, Rockefeller flew into town and I met him at the airport and encouraged him to spend a few hours in Harlem. His aides didn't want him to waste his time in Harlem, but Rocky thought it was a good idea. So I walked Rocky and his entourage up and down the avenue. By the time we got to the Apollo, there was a line around the block. James Brown was playing that night. I don't believe Nelson Rockefeller knew from James Brown. At least he didn't when we arrived. But by the time we left, he knew all about him.

As soon as we got out of the car, Rocky told his guys: "Get coffee for all these people." And so the aides went looking for a coffee shop they could buy out, and I began walking Nelson Rockefeller down the line. Rocky went down the block, shaking hands, greeting the people. I took Rockefeller around to the 126th Street stage door and into the theatre. During the show, Rockefeller walked onstage and paid homage to the hardest-working man in soul business. Rocky and James did the boogaloo on stage and tore the theatre up.

Nina Simone, who sang a requiem for Dr. King the night he was martyred, was known as a "difficult" artist. But she is a wonderful singer, a woman with true blues soul.

James gave him the microphone and Rockefeller said, "I'd like to stay and see your entire show, but I got an election coming up in the morning and I got to go out and get some votes."

The next day, Rockefeller won reelection with the largest black vote he ever got up in Harlem.

A lot of people wondered how a staunch Democrat like me could support the Republican son of a robber baron—especially when they knew some of my other political affiliations. Not that my political

The star of Speaker's Corner in Harlem—the southwest corner of Seventh Avenue and 125th Street—was one of the greatest orators of the twentieth century: Malcolm X (né Malcolm Little), former Lindy Hopper, Pullman porter, and pot runner who turned on most of the great bop musicians of the era before he became one of Harlem's most eloquent voices. Malcolm is at right, leaning on the phone booth; the little boy by my side is Ralph II. The Malcolm I knew preached justice, dignity, respect, love, and intelligence, not hate. He should be remembered as a great African-American, whose death was a tragic loss for all America.

background was radical. I call it progressive. I supported Adam Clayton Powell throughout his political career—and Martin Luther King, who was almost assassinated right here in Harlem. He was stabbed by some crazy lunatic woman. It happened in Blumstein's Department Store, across the street from the Apollo. She stabbed him in the chest just missing his heart by a fraction of an inch.

Whenever MLK was in town, he often came to the Apollo and I would introduce him to the audience. People loved him. He would walk out onstage and the whole theatre seemed electrified by his presence. People wanted to be near him, to see him and to touch him. I helped produce an album of his speech from the March on Washington. I still have a large tape archive on Dr. King, from his speeches and interviews.

I'd say that behind Dr. King, the most powerful political voice of the sixties belonged to Malcolm X, a former Pullman porter and waiter who was friends with many of the musicians and performers who worked at the Apollo. Malcolm was a helluva dancer—he was one of the regular Lindy Hoppers at the Savoy Ballroom, where you could still go Lindy Hopping in the 1940s and into the 1950s. Malcolm made money on the side as a pot runner. He used to sell rolled-up reefers to musicians at the Apollo. After doing time in prison, Malcolm changed his life around. He stopped selling pot and began pushing a new black pride as the spokesperson for the Muslims. He became known as Malcolm X.

At the time, I was very friendly with Muhammad Ali, who used to stand up and take a bow whenever he was at the Apollo to see a show or attend Amateur Night backstage. Malcolm was friendly with Muhammad because he had helped bring him into the movement. Malcolm and Ali were planning to do a benefit at the Apollo and they wanted me to participate. We did the benefit. I then wrote and recorded an album for Malcolm entitled, "The Bullet or the Ballot." It discussed the Dr. King philosophy of nonviolence and the Malcolm X philosophy of an "eye for an eye."

Malcolm was a great, great orator. He wasn't the hate monger the government made him out to be. He was fighting for what he saw as the rights of black people. From his own experience, he believed white society victimized all black families. That's because every single man in his family—his father, his brothers, his uncles—had died a violent death. Malcolm believed they were victims of a racist society. That, and his experiences in jail, influenced everything he said.

I think Malcolm appealed to a large number of black people because he was absolutely fearless. He would really stir people up. He talked fast and he always had full command of what he was going to say. No slow southern-preacher thing for Malcolm. He was a machine gun.

Toward the end of his life, Malcolm broke with Elijah Muhammad's nation of Islam that called for a separation of the races. Malcolm traveled to Mecca and met other Muslims who practiced a more fundamental and Orthodox Islam that stressed brotherhood between black and white. He came to the realization that this was not a restrictive religion for black or dark races, it was for all races. When he came home, he spoke about his new insights. (He broke with the Honorable Elijah Muhammad, and it is alleged that was why he was killed.)

The day that Malcolm was shot, I was going up to the Audubon Ballroom on Broadway at 166th Street, where he was holding meetings every Sunday. I was going to talk on Malcolm's behalf, to encourage people to make donations to Malcolm's cause. Malcolm didn't like to ask for money himself, so I told him I would make the pitch for him. Malcolm said, "That would be great, Coop, and I appreciate it. I'll have them call you to let you know when to come up. That way you won't be sitting around all day, waiting to come on and speak."

So I was home when the phone rang. It was a woman at the Audubon. She said, "Malcolm wanted me to tell you that any time now you—" Suddenly I heard this sound over the phone—*bop, bop, bop, bop.* I didn't know what it was. It sounded like somebody was throwing stones at a microphone or setting off firecrackers inside a snare-drum head. I said, "What is that? What is going on?"

The woman started screaming into the phone. "My God—my God! Malcolm is shot! Somebody shot Malcolm!"

"Shot him? Somebody shot Malcolm?"

Then she dropped the phone, and I could hear screams and shouts and people running. Then the phone went dead.

The Audubon is right across the street from Columbia Presbyterian Medical Center and they wheeled Malcolm to the hospital, but he was DOA.

Nowadays people talk about the sixties as an era of great romance and excitement that witnessed the birth of a new age in American history. In reality, America was a segregated, uptight, and sexist society that had to choose between radical change or self-destruction. For a time it looked as if a second civil war was going to break out—not between North and South but between young and old, hip and square, poor and rich, black and white.

In the end, the country seemed to grow up. But it was a brutal time. And the despair was felt in my house too. One morning I woke up and it seemed as if the afflictions of the land were visited upon me. One half of my face was frozen—paralyzed. The other half was

Some of our great female vocalists, who kept the spirit of the Apollo alive through good times and bad: Roberta Flack (*top*), Natalie Cole (*left*), and Melba Moore.

normal. My face was at war. It felt as if half my head was alive and the other half was asleep. When I tried to smile, my mouth turned down instead of up. I looked in the mirror and it was as if my eye was about to pop out of my head. I looked like one of those theatre masks—one side of my face was comedy, the other side was tragedy. This would have been fine if I was in the advertising business. I could have rented my face out by the week. Since I was a performer, facial paralysis could mean the final curtain of my career. My face is my living. If I can't mug and smile, I can't act.

Mucho grande ladies of the Apollo, past and present: Chaka Khan, Davita, and Nancy Wilson.

Needless to say, I didn't take this downturn of events sitting. I told myself not to worry until I talked to my doctor. That's when I really started to worry. I had been stricken with something known as Bell's palsy, the doc said. Facial muscles, he said, are controlled by two nerves, one on each side of the face. The nerves run from the brain to the face through a little hole behind the ear. If either of those

More Apollo favorites (*clockwise from upper left*): Carmen McRae, Millie Jackson, Lonette McKee, and Gwen Guthrie.

nerves gets pinched, paralysis can occur. The doc said nobody knows how the nerves get pinched. They think it may be related to infection in the inner ear, which can cause swelling in the nearby nerve tissue. When the nerve swells as it emerges from the skull near the ear, it can become pinched.

Oh, yes—there was one other small detail, the doctor said:

Vive la femme (clockwise from upper left): Stephanie Mills, Anita Baker, Regina Belle, and Karyn White.

''There's no treatment for Bell's palsy.'' There was nothing he could do for me, he said, except to say that because my eye looked and felt like it was about to pop out of my head, I had to be sure to keep it moistened with eye drops. My blinking reflex had lost its reflex. I couldn't blink my eye, but I could see that there wasn't much use for a TV host with a paralyzed face or an emcee who couldn't laugh, cry, or talk without slurring. The bottom line was that they don't know what causes Bell's palsy and they don't know how long it lasts. But they don't consider it life-threatening, either. So I knew it wasn't terribly dangerous—just damned embarrassing.

As much as I would have enjoyed sitting around the house feeling sorry for myself, I never got the chance to face the music. I worked hard at therapy, did lots of writing, prayed, and enjoyed my family, who were loving and supportive, especially my wife, Betti.

A mutual friend got word to Governor Rockefeller that I was out of work. Rocky remembered getting his Coops' Tour of Harlem on election eve a few years back. And as a politician, it was his business to return favors. So a few weeks after I woke up with my contorted face, Rocky himself called me up and said, "Coop, I hear you hung up your star down at the Apollo. Well, I hate to think of you enjoying yourself too much, and I know you're too young for retirement, so I was wondering if you would do me a favor?"

"You name it, Governor," I said.

"Coop, I wonder if you would do me and the state of New York the honor of serving as director of information for the State Division of Human Rights? Go on down to 270 Broadway, to the State Office Building. I've taken the liberty of putting your name on the door down there."

So that's how it happened that when people rang me up at work, my secretary would say, "Governor's office." Friends started calling me Governor Cooper. "Didn't know Rocky died and made you governor, Coop."

Basically, the job involved me in civil rights disputes and other urban affairs. If someone felt he or she was discriminated against, by the police or any executive branch of the state government, I would mediate the dispute. In time, my facial paralysis cleared up and I was able to get back onstage and host Amateur Night now and then. But for the better part of those years, I played a game called politics, which is part show and part business. When Rockefeller resigned to run for President, Malcolm Wilson became governor, and my position was secured. Same with Hugh Carey and Mario Cuomo. But by the time Mario got in there, I was itching to get back to my first love. So, in order to get back to the world of show business, I resigned. And just in time, too.

Dark Lights, Big Future

★ ★

THE DEATH AND REBIRTH OF RALPH COOPER'S ORIGINAL HARLEM AMATEUR NIGHT

The 1970s were not exactly a golden age for live entertainment—in Harlem or anywhere else. Discos made stars of the deejays—the record spinners, not the record makers. The disco sound was a "black sound" in the beginning, but the old pattern held: the Bee Gees, a white group, became the biggest name in popular music.

There was no event more symbolic of the cultural decay of the age than the tragedy that occurred in 1977, when the Apollo Theatre, aged forty-three, died of neglect. It was as if Harlem's own heart stopped. You could almost hear the life go out of the community.

The end began years earlier. Before he died, in January 1974, Frank Schiffman began liquidating his real estate holdings in Harlem. He sold off a string of theatres, including the Lafayette, the Lincoln, the Odeon, the Renaissance, the Roosevelt, to religious organizations—which guaranteed they would never reopen as theatres, because a theatre makes a great church, and rarely will one stray from that higher, tax-exempt, calling. The pattern was followed by the RKO and Loews theatres. I think if Frank Schiffman really cared about black entertainment, he never would have sold out to church interests, which paid top dollar. It was a great investment for the church, but it was devilish bad news for anyone interested in preserving the arts in Harlem, not to mention the artists. Schiffman never got around to selling the Apollo, though he tried to interest a sale. Today, the only theatre other than the Apollo that doesn't belong to a religious organization is the Roosevelt on Seventh Avenue at 145th Street. That grand old theatre is a Pioneer supermarket now.

When Schiffman died, *Variety* marked his passing by noting, erroneously, that "before his acquisition of the Apollo, black patronage was shunned." The fact is, the Apollo was presenting black entertainment for black audiences from the first day it opened, early in 1934. And I was there to help raise the curtain, not Schiffman, who didn't take over until the spring of 1935.

After Schiffman's death, the despair that had seemed to descend over Harlem in the wake of Dr. King's assassination and the so-called riots his murder sparked remained. But the Apollo, and especially the amateur show, remained beacons of promise. Folks may have been afraid to walk the streets of Harlem in those days, but that didn't keep them from going out on Wednesday nights to catch the rising and falling stars at the Apollo.

The Schiffman and Brecker families, which bought the Apollo, vowed to keep it going as a first-rate theatre. But business wasn't good. Conditions inside were as depressing as ever. And the feeling of security audiences had had disappeared in 1975 when two gunslingers staged an OK Corral shootout in the balcony during a Smokey Robinson concert. This was not good for business, to say the least.

In 1978, a year after the Schiffman family finally closed the theatre, my worst dreams came true when his son Bobby announced that the family was negotiating a sale of the Apollo to a church group. Luckily, they picked a problem buyer: three years later, the family repossessed the Apollo after the church fell behind on its payments. Later, the Schiffmans found another buyer in the religious community. But again there was a glitch in the deal; and while the problem was being worked out, I arranged a meeting between Walter Brecker, Leo's son, and an interested buyer, Lloyd Dickens, a black Harlem millionare who was unable to contact the Apollo ownership. Then, like a rainbow that appears after a violent storm, my brother Percy Sutton entered the scene. (We're not blood brothers, but we're that close.) Percy, who chairs Inner City Broadcasting and owns seven radio stations, including WBLS and WLIB in New York, helped block the sale. In 1982 he arranged for the theatre to be taken over by

HUDC—the Harlem Urban Development Corporation, a state agency—which then leased the theatre to Percy's people. If that hadn't happened, the Apollo would have become a church and remained a church for as long as it stands.

In July 1983, the Apollo became a National Historic Landmark, which means Harlem's oldest functioning theatre can never be destroyed, except by fire, earthquake, or some other act of God—which isn't likely to happen, since it's well known that the Deity digs hot sounds, especially soul music.

Though the Apollo was spared the fate of its sister theatres and remained a secular showcase, it is truly a place of worship. At the Apollo, an amateur performer's prayers—not only for stardom but simply to be the best that he can be—are answered.

Chairman Sutton has worked miracles of his own. Under his direction, the Apollo, where generations of performers and audiences suffocated in summer and froze in winter, has been completely renovated and refurbished. Today it is one of the most beautiful theatres in the world, with a mirrored lobby, gorgeous chandeliers, plush red wall coverings, and new box seats, trimmed in gold. The dressing rooms have been rebuilt and refurbished, modern bathrooms have been installed, and the theatre has been equipped with elevators as well as new heating and air-conditioning systems. The theatre has been entirely rewired and rigged with state-of-the-art recording facilities and a full complement of film and video equipment.

When the Irish superstars U2 shot their hit video "Angel of Harlem" at the Apollo, they took advantage of in-house facilities that rival those of any sound stage or recording studio in the country. And our acoustics, like our legend, can't be duplicated anywhere, for any price.

Creative booking and management policies have made the theatre a resounding success, with motion-picture premieres, benefit concerts, and showcases by the likes of Aretha Franklin, Hall and Oates, Jonathan Butler, Lionel Richie, and Stevie Wonder. Such new stars as Al B. Sure!, Keith Sweat, Big Daddy Kane, and Bobby Brown, Run-D.M.C. have all appeared at the new, revitalized Apollo. The theatre is still the pinnacle.

When the Apollo went dark, I didn't have time to fret over my job. I worked steadily on radio throughout the 1970s and until the

Apollo reopened. I had a successful consulting firm, which is why I resigned my job with the state—I had more work than I could handle.

I enjoyed deejaying. It's like being emcee—without the live audience. My show on WOV was popular for a segment we did during the last half-hour, at two-thirty a.m. each night.

We called it "Work Time." That's when I'd play the beautiful music, the slow and romantic stuff by Sinatra and Streisand and Lou Rawls, Eckstine, Prysock, Dinah Washington, and other fine singers. It wasn't dance music; it was music for lovers to do their "work" to. "Work time" is when you get together with whomever you're with and you turn the lights down low and go to work. I talked soft and slow and the music was sexy and the rest is up to the listeners, you dig?

Through the seventies, the eighties, and now the nineties, the O'Jays just keep on hitting. Eddie Levert and the lads began the new decade as surprise winners of an American Music Award.

For me, the hardest part of the Apollo's closing was knowing that throughout Harlem there were talented young people being deprived of the opportunity to make their dreams come true.

It was impossible to know how many kids were out there with their dreams unfulfilled. It kept eating at me—how many young Ella Fitzgeralds and Bill Kennys and Michael Jacksons and Sarah Vaughans were singing and dancing in their basements and bedrooms, waiting for a shot that might never come? All I knew was that there were a helluva lot of them. For fifty years we maintained long waiting lists of would-be amateurs hungry for a chance to prove themselves. During those long years the Apollo was closed, how many future stars missed the opportunity to prove their valor, to test their nerve, to strut their stuff? How many gave up their dreams? How many still doubt themselves?

I had plenty of time to reflect on the meaning of Amateur Night during what I called the theatre's Dark Ages. (It certainly seemed like it was closed for ages.) What brilliant insight did I gain? Just this:

One of the first acts Chairman Percy E. Sutton performed after he helped buy and reopen the Apollo Theatre was to resurrect Ralph Cooper's Harlem Amateur Night show. For that burst of show-business genius, I am forever grateful.

Here is the Chairman as he appeared with his family and Congressman Charles Rangel during his unsuccessful bid for the mayoralty of New York City, later won by his dear friend and business partner, David Dinkins.

that the importance of Amateur Night wasn't that we launched so many future stars toward the heavens, or that Amateur Night helped make the Apollo Theatre the leading showcase for black entertainment. What was most important was that we gave thousands of young people the opportunity to learn something profound about themselves and some lessons about life itself. Some discovered that they would never solo on Broadway. They learned the hard way that they weren't the next Marian Anderson or Paul Robeson. Fame and fortune don't await every kid who walks out on the stage on Wednesday nights. But wisdom might.

When the Apollo Theatre closed, the hopes of a generation of young people went dark with it. And when I heard from Chairman Sutton that the Apollo was going to reopen, in December 1983, fifty years and one month after Clarence Robinson and I left the Lafayette to sign on at the new 125th Street Apollo Theatre, I was elated. And when the chairman asked me to inaugurate the reborn theatre with a new edition of Ralph Cooper's Original Harlem Amateur Night, it was one of the happiest moments of my life.

The format for Amateur Night has gone through many changes. In the beginning, we had contestants touch the varnished piece of the Tree of Hope on their way to the stage. Later we had contestants do the Truck as they came offstage—the side-shuffle step Pigmeat used to do as an exit step, waving one finger in the air.

Now, in the new and improved Amateur Night, we have the Club Apollo format. After intermission, we raise the curtain on a nightclub set reminiscent of yesterday's Harlem. We have a team of gorgeous models—men and women—sitting at tables arranged as if they were stage-side at the old Cotton Club or Small's Paradise or Connie's Inn or any one of Harlem's outstanding clubs.

Now that the variety-show format is a thing of the past—no chorus lines, which we all miss, but no twenty-eight-show-a-week grind, either—we can't offer amateur winners a week-long engagement at the Apollo. So what we do is have the top four winners of every Wednesday-night competition return to compete in a special Show Offs amateur contest, held every four weeks. Then, every three months, the Show Off winners compete in the Top Dog contest. Then the top four winners from each of the three Top Dog contests are invited to compete in the annual Super Dog competition. Super Dog is the biggest show of the year, and it's held just before New Year's. We have contestants coming in from all over the country for Super Dog. We've had kids from about every state in the union, plus Germany, France, England, and Japan.

Our 1986 Super Dog winner was a young man named David Peaston, a church singer from St. Louis, by way of Brooklyn, who is as fine a vocalist as I've ever heard at the Apollo. David sings Billie Holiday's "God Bless the Child." Now that's Billie's song and always will be; but I swear, David Peaston has made that song his, too. So maybe the two of them can share it.

David has music in his genes. His sister is the fabulous Fontella Bass, who wrote and performed one of the classic million-selling hits of the sixties, "Rescue Me." The first time I saw David was at a

Ralph II was working at WKTU radio when Cher dropped by to say hello. This was back in the early eighties, just before she began to pump iron.

Monday-night audition. It was a real cattle call, held in a tiny re-. hearsal hall. There must have been five hundred people crammed into that tiny space. In order to get through all those people, we were rushing folks on- and offstage. No one had time to complete an entire song. Always I listen to a few bars and base my decision on that.

But when David stood and started to sing "God Bless the Child," the entire theatre went quiet. He sang the song all the way through. It was beautiful to listen to. I was anxious to have him on Amateur Night, because I knew he wouldn't have his amateur status for long. But the following Wednesday was booked solid, and there was no place to squeeze him in. So Jackie Smith, my talent coordinator, got his phone number and we promptly lost it. Man, I turned the office upside down looking for that number. Several weeks passed and we

David Peaston (*lower right*) won our 1987 Super Top Dog, Amateur of the Year contest in 1987. In 1989, his first album, *Introducing David Peaston* made the Top Ten of Billboard's Black Albums chart. That's Jimmy "Bright Lights Big City" Reed (*top left*), Fats Domino (*lower left*), and (*upper right*), Luther Vandross, who had a long labor giving birth to his star at the Apollo.

didn't hear from him. When he finally called, I told him we'd been frantic trying to find him. He said he was glad he called. He didn't for all those weeks, he said, because he thought we weren't interested.

When David finally appeared on Amateur Night, he followed someone who had been booed offstage. David is a very big, bulky man, and when he first walked out onstage, some joker yelled ''Barry

White!'' People started laughing, and I was afraid David was going to be unnerved. But he just let the song take over, and his voice filled the theatre. Right away, people were trying to shush the hecklers; a couple of ladies called out "Sing it, baby, sing it!" By the end of the last verse, there was absolute silence in the theatre. Everyone was carried away with the beauty of his singing. And when he finished and took a bow, the hall erupted.

David won that night, and he kept on winning until he was the Super Dog champ that year. Since then, his career has skyrocketed. Soon after he won, he signed a record contract with Geffen Records, and in 1989 he released his first album, *Introducing David Peaston*. His very first single, "Two Wrongs (Don't Make It Right)," was a Top 5 smash on the rhythm-and-blues charts and a Top 40 pop hit.

David taped the video for "Two Wrongs" at the Apollo, and whenever he's in town, he drops by. He's an inspiration to the kids down in the Green Room. The kids are always worried about the audience, and David usually says, "It's an honest crowd. If they like you, they'll get behind you. If they don't, they're not going to fake it. Amateur Night," David says, "is the true acid test. If you want to know where you stand, the audience out there tonight will gladly let you know."

Another big recent winner is a young fellow named Billy Robinson, who landed a record contract after winning the Wednesday-night festivities. Billy is partially blind and he has a heart full of soul. He has a rich baritone voice that is a cross between the young Billy Eckstine and Arthur Prysock. He has a real gift that mixes the spirituality of gospel and the earthy, bluesy, sexy feel you want to hear in pop. Billy's another one with a big future ahead of him.

In the old days, people like Jack Benny, Bob Hope, Eddie Cantor, Jackie Gleason, and Joe Louis used to be surprise guests on the amateur hour. Now the people who come out and take a bow and wow the crowd are young stars like Keith Sweat, who grew up in the projects right up 125th Street, and Al B. Sure! and Bobby Brown, Mike Tyson, Spike Lee, Special Ed, and Big Daddy Kane. The crowd loves it when these people appear, just like they loved it thirty and forty years ago when the big radio stars took a bow.

Luther Vandross is one of the new generation of pop singers who braved the Amateur Night audience and won. But it was a big struggle for Luther, and he almost didn't make it. Luther is a local boy with

Continuing a superstar tradition, Jackie Jackson greets fans at an outdoor production of our "Salute to Harlem."

a wonderful talent. He'd always been a gifted singer, but he never ventured far from church. When he first began to sing in public, he got nervous easy. He has a gentle nature and he used to get spooked, like a young horse gets spooked by a sudden noise—he'll kick and jump and fidget and nobody can keep a saddle on him. Same with Luther. He'd rehearse a song 10,000 times and get it just right 9,999 times. But as soon as he walked out in front of that audience and saw those kids hanging from the rafters in the balcony, he'd bolt and run.

Luther was run off this stage four times in a row. Four times he'd come out and start his song and he'd jump the key. I told him, it happened to Ella Fitzgerald; it can happen to the best. Just settle down. I told him what they tell players in the NBA—play inside yourself, play your own game. But it didn't do any good. Luther just could not handle that audience. I thought he would quit. I thought four times is too many times to go through that hurt. I'd seen too many talented, exquisitely talented kids give it up because they couldn't lick that stage fright. They couldn't handle the jolt. That adrenaline kicks through your body like an electric charge. You got to be able to handle that, and if you can't, my advice is to hang it up.

I thought Luther was one of the ones who couldn't find the calm in the storm that began to rage through him every time he walked out onstage. It was a shame too, because he could sing awhile. He was fantastic backstage, in rehearsals with the band, down in the Green Room warming up. People would stop what they were doing just to listen to him. But out there in front of the jury, he got the chair every time.

By the fifth time, the audience knew Luther when he walked out, and I could tell they were itching to boo him again. But this time, Luther was a changed man. He came out and the band struck up his tune and he hit the right key and he got in the groove and the dude moved everybody in the house. Luther killed them that night. He won the show in a walk, and it seemed a month had barely passed when his first album was out and climbing the charts.

The irony is, Luther's success backfired on us. We wanted to use Luther to help promote the theatre. Luther's people got back to us and said their boy would be happy to play the Apollo as a headliner. He would do two shows, just as we asked. But he would only do a half-hour each time out, and he wanted $400,000 for the engagement. That's $200,000 per half-hour of work. I agreed he should get it. But this was an offer the theatre had to refuse. They said, "Thanks, Mr. Vandross, but no thanks." I guess he was thinking about all the nights he got booed instead of the night he won. And I can understand that. People say you get booed by the Apollo audience and never forget it. You hear those boos in your head for the rest of your life.

Just as Luther Vandross heard all about Ella Fitzgerald's problems with the audience, now I tell Luther's story to reassure contestants who doubt they have what it takes.

We had a singer one week who flew all the way in from Los Angeles on the day of the show. I never saw the guy or heard him sing before he went on. I never even talked to him. His wife called me on Monday night from California and said she wanted to fly in

Pieces of a Dream is a contemporary Apollo act with a bright future.

with her husband who was a wonderful singer, and more than anything in the world he wanted to sing at the Apollo.

I said, "Well, you understand, ma'am, that we have a heavy competition here. If he's not a good singer, I'd hate for you to spend all that money on plane tickets just to get booed and run offstage."

"Oh, no, Mr. Cooper," she said, "we know all about your amateur show, and we wouldn't want to be on it if we didn't think we could win. My husband is a wonderful singer."

"Well, why not wait a few weeks and come out when you can get a discount on your plane tickets?"

She was quiet for a second, and then she sounded a little embarrassed. "We already bought our tickets, Mr. Cooper. That's why we have to get on tomorrow night's show."

What could I do? I said, "In that case, come on and we'll make room for you."

She said they'd be there Wednesday night.

I knew only one of two things could happen: he could be great and win the contest and maybe become a star, or he could get run offstage. But I thought it was a damn shame if he came all the way from California for that. I told his wife all this, so my responsibility was done. But still, I worried.

When I saw the young man next day, my worries left me. He was a big, tall, handsome fella dressed in a beautiful white suit. I thought, "Man, this guy looks good. He looks like a winner." I gave him a big introduction since he'd flown all that way—"Direct from California . . ." He looked great walking out there.

He found the spotlight and he picked up the mike and he opened his mouth. I don't think he got past four bars before the audience started. Man, they gave it to him. I did everything I could to keep him out there. But the audience spoke—loud and clear. He got the siren, the band kicked in, and Lacey, the Executioner, came on in full regalia and chased him off with a pistol and a bullwhip and a popgun. At least he got the full treatment.

When he went off, he went downstairs and changed his clothes, and he and his wife came up to my dressing room at intermission. I told him I felt bad about what happened. I said maybe he should have come in time for the rehearsal. They said next time they would. They were real nice about it. I shook his hand and he said, "Thanks, Mr. Cooper, for having me here. It was a pleasure."

I thought, "A pleasure?" What a nice guy! Most people who get booed off come back and find me and they say, "You got an awful audience out there. They're horrible. You can take 'em and shove 'em!" But this guy got the treatment and came back to tell me how much he enjoyed it. So I said, "Well, what are you two going to do now? I guess you'll be spending a few days in the city? Is this your first time in the Big Apple?"

"No," he said, "we've got to catch a cab back to the airport."

They got a cab and went on back to California that night. It was the damndest thing. He arrived on Wednesday, got to the theatre at five-thirty, got booed off by nine, hopped a cab to the airport, and—boom—back to California on the red-eye. I never heard from the guy again.

I wonder if I had heard him audition if I could have predicted what was going to happen. Usually you can come closer to saying who's going to be great than to tell who will be booed off.

One week a woman flew in from Memphis with her seven-year-old daughter. The little girl's whole ambition was to perform at the Apollo, the woman said. I wondered if it wasn't really the mother's ambition. "How will she react if she gets booed?" I said.

"She's prepared for that," the mother said. "She knows she could possibly get booed offstage."

That night, when I introduced the little girl, I said, "This young lady wanted so badly to come here from Tennessee and entertain you. Finally her parents brought her up to the Apollo as a Christmas present." I brought her onstage and she was such a cute little girl. I was so delighted because the audience accepted her. She wasn't a real prime singer, but everybody was polite. Some even threw money. I really loved the audience that week. I told 'em so, too. "I could just hug and kiss every one of you," I said.

Many times in rehearsal one of my production assistants will take aside a performer who is struggling and say, "Look, you need to rehearse more. Work on your number and get your act down just like you want it and come back in a few weeks and audition again." We try not to discourage the kids, because they can develop tremendously with a little more practice. But we also don't want to send somebody out there who we know is going to get rough treatment and who may not be able to handle it.

Years ago we had a kid named Anthony Gourdine who wanted to be on the show, but he got himself so tied up in knots, he couldn't even handle the audition. He was so nervous he couldn't remember the words, his mouth was dry, and he was shaking in his socks. And this was with just a few people sitting around listening. There was no way he could handle the real Apollo audience. He might have a nervous breakdown out there. So we told him, as gently as possible, to come back later.

Anthony never did make it as an amateur. But two years after

Four superstars of today (*clockwise from top left*): Freddie Jackson, Keith Sweat, Al B. Sure!, and Big Daddy Kane.

that audition he made his professional debut at the Apollo as Little Anthony of Little Anthony and the Imperials.

In the last half-century, I've lived through half a dozen eras of American culture, from swing and bebop to R&B, rock and roll, soul, disco, funk, and rap. As great as each of those creative periods has been, I think this current era, in many ways, is the most exciting of all. The talent of today is more vigorous and more energetic than ever before. Whenever I walk downstairs into the Green Room on Amateur Night, I see Harlem's bright future in the eyes of all those eager young beautiful brothers and sisters.

This is an especially exciting time because black artists have never so completely dominated popular music as they do now. From Michael Jackson, Janet Jackson, Prince, Bobby Brown, Whitney Houston, Anita Baker, Aretha Franklin, Patti LaBelle, Gladys Knight, Stephanie Mills, Harry Belafonte, and on down, black acts are the biggest things in show business today. Black music provides the sound track for our lives. Radio, television, movies, even commercials on TV—they all use music by black artists to stir emotions, to entertain, and even to educate.

"Crossover" today is almost meaningless. The big acts all break into the pop charts, even rap stars like L.L. Cool J, Run-D.M.C., Tone-Loc, Doug E. Fresh, Big Daddy Kane, Biz Markie, Eric B and Rakim, Heavy D, Salt 'N Pepa—the list goes on and on. Today's young black artists aren't sharecropping. They're managing their own careers and their own lives. You can be sure Al B. Sure!, Paula Abdul, and Bobby Brown aren't going to get ripped off like Bessie Smith, Ma Rainey, Little Richard, Otis Blackwell, Ruth Brown, and all the others who were. These young new artists won't be denied, because they have learned from the mistakes of those who went before. They've bothered to learn the business half of show business, which is what I've been preaching to Harlem's young performers for fifty years. This business isn't all show. If you think it is, you're going to be crying all the way to the welfare office.

When kids come along and do well on Amateur Night, I always try to stay close enough to them to help them. Big mistakes can be made very early in a young career. I talk to the kids to find out who their managers are and make sure that they cut a deal that is to their best advantage monetarily, artistically, and psychologically. Everyone needs a manager. You can't do it alone. That's something every performer has to learn, and I stress this as soon as I see someone has a future in show business.

Throughout this century, just about every important trend in American popular culture began as a phenomenon in the black show-business community. In the past, those trends were always absorbed

Our fifth annual "Salute to Harlem" included these happy fans and a pair of Lindy Hoppers, demonstrating the most exhilarating dance ever.

and "whitened." Today, we have black artists who are capitalizing on the popularity of black dances and music and comedy.

Today there is an unprecedented amount of room at the top for successful black performers. But the sad thing is that there are few middle rungs on the ladder to the top.

I don't think an all-around song and dance man like myself would have many places to go in today's overall show-business world. For many of today's kids, the Apollo is the zenith, the show-business ultimate. With a real theatrical circuit, there's no training ground for

Nine-year-old Michelle Watson and big sister Myiia, eleven, came all the way from Washington, D.C., to compete in our 1990 Amateur of the Year, Super Top Dog contest. It was worth the trip—the Watson Sisters became the 1990 Amateurs of the Year.

young black talents, especially novelty-type acts. Some of the greatest stars in show-business history started out as novelty acts. W. C. Fields was nothing but a gifted juggler. Fred Astaire and his sister did some trick dancing on vaudeville, and Fred became the King of Hollywood. Today, where would talents like those go to learn and grow? Except for the one-in-a-million talent, there are precious few career paths open.

One week we had an amateur contortionist on the show. I hadn't seen an act like this since those Chicago World's Fair freaks were on fifty years before. Our audience had never seen anything like this kid's act. He was unbelievable. He didn't walk out onstage—he rolled. He was all twisted up like a pretzel, with his feet around his neck and his rear end where you'd expect his stomach to be. At first, the audience thought he was deformed. There was a tension in the theatre: "What the hell is Cooper doing—bringing a cripple out for us to laugh at?" But then he straightened himself out bit by bit and twisted himself into different shapes, and the audience just went nuts.

His was a great act, but what sort of future does a contortionist have in today's world? One night on David Letterman's Stupid Human Tricks and then a sideshow gig in Las Vegas. If he's lucky, he'll only have to work a part-time day job to make the rent.

Possibly the future of show business is in the home, like the TV executives say. Perhaps that will be the next step for Ralph Cooper's Harlem Amateur Night show. I can see a day when home entertainment systems allow home viewers to help pick the winners and losers onstage at the Apollo. We would keep the Executioner format, of course, but find a way to create competition between the theatre audience and the home audience. Maybe viewers could call in their boos or cheers or punch them in on Q computers.

My dream would be to see my son, Ralph II, who is currently my cohost and right arm, become emcee after me and carry the tradition into the twenty-first century. "The Original Harlem Amateur Night Hosted by Ralph Cooper II." That would make me eternally happy, to have the tradition of Amateur Night pass from one generation to the next, and to know that we were offering opportunity to the next generation of talented young people the world over.

I can't help thinking that Amateur Night in Harlem will outlive me and Ralph II and the yet-to-be-born Ralph Cooper III. The fact

I'm already grooming my grandson Wayne, who likes to call himself "Ralph Cooper the Third," for my job.

is, if it can make it through the Depression and the death of the Harlem Renaissance, World War II, the advent of television, and the end of the golden age of Harlem theatre, through disco and through uptown's bleak economic decline, it can survive any calamity.

Even the Big One.

Index